CREATIVE CAKES

CREATIVE CAKES

Stephanie Crookston

David Obst Books/Random House New York

To my mother, who always cleaned up after me

Library of Congress Cataloging in Publication Data
Crookston, Stephanie, 1947–
Creative cakes.
"David Obst books."
Includes index.
1. Cake. 2. Cake decorating. I. Title.
TX771.C76   641.8'653   77-90311
1SBN 0-394-42499-9

Design by Anne Lian

Illustrations by Christine Swirnoff

Manufactured in the United States of America
24689753
First Edition

Acknowledgments

Thanks to my parents, Don and Carol Crookston. Thanks to Kay Kavanagh, Frank DiGiacomo and Ann Miller. Thanks to Barbara and Jerry Della Femina. Thanks to Jim Penick. Thanks to Bob Giraldi, Dick Raboy, Ron Travisano. And thanks to Kathy Matthews, my editor. These are the talented people who in one way or another have influenced and encouraged me to learn everything I needed to know to make *Creative Cakes* possible.

Special appreciation to all my helpful friends and acquaintances who have supported me throughout the stages of *Creative Cakes*.

Contents

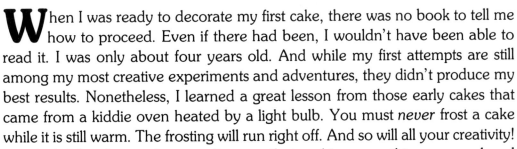

Introduction

When I was ready to decorate my first cake, there was no book to tell me how to proceed. Even if there had been, I wouldn't have been able to read it. I was only about four years old. And while my first attempts are still among my most creative experiments and adventures, they didn't produce my best results. Nonetheless, I learned a great lesson from those early cakes that came from a kiddie oven heated by a light bulb. You must *never* frost a cake while it is still warm. The frosting will run right off. And so will all your creativity!

It didn't take me long to discover that making something personal and original for someone gave me a great feeling of satisfaction. Comments such as "terrific" and "delicious" and "beautiful" quickly taught me that I had happened into a fun and challenging hobby that provided my friends and family (and especially me) with many hours of happiness and gratification through my teenage years.

What's more, by the time I'd finished college and had begun working in the advertising world on Madison Avenue in New York City, friends and friends of friends kept me busier after work with my cake creations than I was during the day at work. (And contrary to what some people think of the advertising industry, at the then-tiny agency where I worked, that meant busy!) After toying with the idea of a cake shop for a couple of years, and after five years of working my way up from creative-department secretary to an advertising copywriter, I took a deep breath and plunged all my savings and some money I borrowed from my parents and several friends into what many considered a half-baked idea. It's now my dream-come-true business called Creative Cakes.

Since Creative Cakes opened its doors in December 1974, I've cut and sculptured cakes into more shapes, sizes and designs than I ever imagined possible. Many of those cakes will be illustrated for you throughout this book; you'll also come upon many "cake stories" that I've found precious and dear. Once you have achieved a few basic skills, you'll find that your creative horizons are unlimited. (My biggest limitation has been the condition of the streets in New York City. Potholes and bumpy rides are not good for sculptured cakes. And being a one-person operation, I don't have time to personally deliver every cake. You'll be able to do much more in your own home, because usually the only traveling your cakes will have to do is from the kitchen to the dining room table.) I'm continually amazed at the ideas that pop into my head, allowing me to create an original cake every time. Once you begin thinking of your cakes as art rather than pastry, there's no reason why anything you can visualize can't be a creative cake—well, almost anything.

It's taken me twenty-five years to develop a style of cake decorating I prefer to call "cake art." *Creative Cakes* is full of all the basic methods, "tricks" and "secrets" I've come to master using completely edible cake and decoration. They are simple practices. And with but a few exceptions, most of the tools and utensils I use to decorate my cakes will already be part of your kitchen.

The real joy of my cake art is that I'm not hampered by hundreds of decorating techniques, many of which are strictly repetitious and mechanical, such as the techniques taught in most cake-decorating courses. None of the common flowers or fancy borders will be featured in this book. I don't mean to disparage these traditional techniques, for they can produce beautiful cakes. I've spent hours with my nose pressed against bakery windows admiring the intricate work on traditional wedding cakes or in *spun* marzipan shapes, an amazing art that is virtually lost today. It's simply that those traditional techniques are not my style. Very few of my cakes are round or square or layered. And if they are, it's because the concept so dictates. Traditional "surface-type" decorations seldom have a place on my cakes. Instead, I enjoy using my imagination and ingenuity to come up with unusual shapes and oftentimes three-dimensional cakes. And I like to use candies such as molded marzipan, gumdrops, licorice laces and Tootsie Rolls for the extra parts on my cakes. I'll show you how to use them, too. Soon you'll find that when you really use your imagination, it's much more fun to shape baseball players from candy than to stick plastic men on your cake. And on and on and on.

While it's true that someone without any artistic ability at all will have a bit of trouble mastering the more elaborate cakes, there will be designs in this book simple enough for anyone who enjoys baking. If you have the desire and the patience, you can do it. And you will enjoy the additional challenge of expressing your creativity in frosting rather than in a lot of fancy baking. It just takes practice. And practice takes time. You may spend a whole day on your first cake. Just keep your initial efforts as simple as possible.

In time, you may even find, as I did, that there are occasions when you'd rather be decorating a cake than doing almost anything else. It will become a high priority on your list of favorite pastimes. After a few oohs and ahs, you'll be hooked on one of the most rewarding hobbies ever. What's more, your friends will begin to eagerly await the arrival of you and your precious cakes on *every* special occasion. They'll love you for your thoughtfulness and ingenuity. And eventually you too will be able to bake cakes for fun and profit if you want to, even if it's out of your own home. And who knows, maybe someday you'll also want to open your very own cake shop.

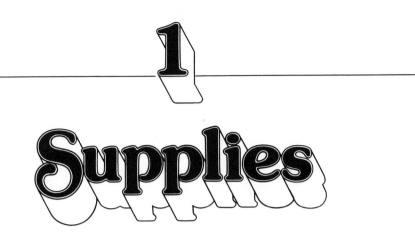

1

Supplies

If you have ever had any interest in cake decorating, you probably already have most of the supplies, utensils and equipment you need to make Creative Cakes. Any of the supplies recommended in this chapter that you need to buy can be purchased in a hardware store or the kitchenwares section of a large department store or supermarket. If for some reason you are not able to find some of the items listed, see page 12 for information on where you can purchase them by mail order.

BAKING EQUIPMENT

Mixer. Your biggest investment in baking will probably be your mixer, assuming that your kitchen is equipped with a stove and a refrigerator. A good mixer is essential. I highly recommend the make my grandmother, mother and I have used with great satisfaction. It's made by KitchenAid, which is a division of Hobart, the most trusted name in mixers throughout the commercial baking industry. The KitchenAid model I'm most familiar with is the K-45. It's a 4½-quart mixer, and unless you're planning to make more than one large cake at a time every time you bake, it's all the mixer you'll ever need. There is another KitchenAid model, the K-5A, that's slightly larger, holding five quarts of mixture.

I used the KitchenAid for a year in my home and every day all day long for over two years in my shop before I had any trouble with it. The speed control went first. And I finally burned out the gears. But I used that mixer more than you'll probably use one in your whole lifetime. When I went to replace it, the salesman talked me into the smallest commercial mixer made by Hobart. It allows me to mix triple batches at one time. However, I really miss my smaller mixer when I have only one recipe to mix. The best thing about all the Hobart products is that they have one revolving beater that also rotates along the sides of the bowl. (Most mixers have two stationary rotary beaters.) With this single revolving beater that gets close to the sides, all the ingredients get mixed. Nothing gets missed. Also, the bowl locks into place, as does the mixer head, so you don't have to worry about the bowl spinning off, as other mixing bowls might that also rotate while the beaters rotate. It's safe to say that once you use it and become accustomed to it, you'll never want or need any other mixer again. It even comes with several attachments, including a dough hook, and many other attachments are available.

Cake Pans.   Cake pans come in all different sizes and are usually made of aluminum or glass. I use only shiny metal pans. Glass pans bake more quickly and at lower temperatures—sometimes as much as 25 degrees lower. I feel glass pans are more cumbersome than metal ones, and I also don't like to worry about breakage. If you already have glass pans and are familiar with their baking requirements, there is no need to invest in metal ones. But for your information, the metal pans I use most often are 11 × 17-inch. You can get thirty servings from the pan if you don't cut a shape from it. And nearly thirty servings if you learn to make your paper patterns economically when you design your shaped cakes. However, a 9 × 13-inch oblong pan may be big enough for you if your parties are not so large. I rarely have use for round or square pans, but you may. A few designs in this book call for 8- or 9-inch round pans.

Mixing Bowls.   The 4-quart (plus) mixing bowls that come with your mixer will probably be enough for mixing your cakes and frosting. However, some smaller 1-quart plastic mixing bowls that fit in the palm of your hand will be handy when you're mixing small amounts of colored frosting. In my operation I prefer stainless-steel or plastic bowls with tightly fitting lids for storage.

Cooling Racks.   Racks come in all different sizes. Cooling your cakes is an essential part of cake baking because cakes should be cooled evenly from all sides. If you don't have cooling racks, you may do as I often do when I have more cakes to cool than racks available to put them on. Take an empty rectangular cake pan and set it upright in a cool place. Place your baked cake in its pan crosswise across the empty pan. Or, as someone suggested to me, if your stove has removable burners, they can work well as cooling racks when placed on a counter. You may be enterprising and discover another way to cool your cakes. You can use any method that permits the air to circulate evenly around the pan, thus ensuring that the bottom of the cake cools while the top does. I generally let my cakes cool at least an hour before I remove them from the pan. However, you can remove your cake from its pan after fifteen minutes and place it on a cooling rack, just as long as you do *not* attempt to frost it until it has cooled for at least an hour.

Timer.   My oven has a timer, as do many these days. It's a great reminder and eliminates guesswork and unnecessary door opening while your cake is in the oven. If you don't have a timer, I'd suggest you buy one. You'll find many other uses for it besides baking.

Rubber Spatula.   A rubber spatula is a must for scraping the sides of your mixing bowl as you mix cake batter or frosting. It's also the only way you'll get every last bit of batter or frosting out of the mixing bowl.

Sifter. Sifters come in all sizes and shapes, none of which have ever held up for a very long time in my kitchen. After years of watching a variety of sifters, from the cheapest to the most expensive, break down before my eyes— seems the crank or the squeezer would always come loose—I finally discovered that an 8-inch sieve—the finer the screen the better—which I shake over a large mixing bowl works just as well. You should remember, however, that my baking is very basic. Fine, delicate baking may require a fine sifter with two or three screens for the best results. Still, I must admit, I've never had any baking failures from my sifting method.

Measuring Cups and Spoons. You'll need a standard set of graduated dry measuring cups and spoons. You'll need a 2-cup dry measuring cup and a 12-cup liquid measuring cup with a pouring spout. I also have a 4-cup liquid measuring cup. Always level off a dry measuring cup with a knife.

Mixing Spoons. Several long-handled mixing spoons are essential. Wooden spoons are good and strong. You'll also find a few tableware teaspoons will help when mixing small amounts of frosting.

Oven Thermometer. If you have any doubts whatsoever about the accuracy of your oven temperature, buy an oven thermometer at your nearest hardware store. (Make sure it's for the oven. Thermometers for the refrigerator look very similar.) Temperature accuracy is an absolute must in cake baking. Simply hang the oven thermometer on the center rack and adjust the thermostat on your oven accordingly.

Eggbeater/Whisk. An eggbeater of some sort or a wire whisk will often come in handy for beating eggs or mixing a small amount of frosting.

DECORATING EQUIPMENT

Decorating Tips. You've seen the tiny metal tips (sometimes they are plastic) used in pastry decorating many times. They are often sold with a pastry bag or a metal or plastic pastry gun. I use Ateco brand, but other manufacturers also make them (see p. 12). I don't use either the bag or the gun. I use only the tips, which may be purchased individually by number, and I use them with parchment cones I fold myself (see pages 17–19). My Creative Cakes are decorated with only the round-hole tips. The tip with the smallest hole is No. 1; that with the largest, No. 12. There are exceptions: I sometimes use the No. 16 for stars (It came in especially handy during America's Bicentennial!), the No. 68 for leaves in a flower basket and a No.

27 for the scraggly hair on Raggedy Ann. These tips are so inexpensive that if you plan on doing much cake decorating, I suggest you buy a good range of sizes. Remember that though a few manufacturers offer them, all of the sizes are standardized.

Parchment Paper. Creative Cakes uses parchment paper for two purposes. The first is to make the disposable cones that are used with reusable metal tips. Instructions for making these cones are on pages 17–19. The second use for parchment paper is to line cake pans. You simply cut the parchment paper to fit the bottom of the cake pan. You don't need to grease any part of the pan. Don't worry about the sides—you can loosen them with a knife. Eventually I discovered that tracing paper works just as well as parchment for lining pans. (I also experimented with waxed paper, as some cookbooks recommend. But even waxed paper sometimes tears and sticks to the bottom of the cake when you try to remove it from the pan.) Tracing paper is much less expensive than parchment paper. Note, however, that tracing paper doesn't work as well as parchment for cones. Tracing paper is slightly more brittle, and it cracks when the cone is filled with frosting. You can buy tracing paper in any art supply store. It comes in many different-sized pads. I buy 11 × 14-inch pads and cut the paper to fit whatever size pan I'm using. You'll find parchment paper wherever gourmet kitchen utensils are sold. It comes in rectangular sheets, in a continuous roll that can be purchased by the pound, and in precut triangles of varying sizes. I prefer the precut triangles made by Ateco for my parchment cones. They are big enough to hold large amounts of frosting for big jobs and to be cut in half for delicate design work when the big cone is too bulky. I guarantee parchment paper for both purposes. And once you use it to line your pans, you'll never go back to the old grease-and-flour method again.

Cake Boards. I've found that the best and most economical serving boards for my unusual-shaped cakes are made from corrugated cardboard and waxed white freezer paper. If freezer paper is not available, you can use aluminum foil. However, I won't recommend it for two reasons: it often tears when you go to cut and serve your cake, and its shiny look takes away from the design of the cake. I also don't like the look of doilies with cake art. They are too frilly and also detract from the cake. If you are making a very large cake, use two pieces of corrugated cardboard set crosswise on each other for additional strength. If your boards are not strong enough for your cakes, your frosting will crack, especially if you have to transport your creations any distance. You will find freezer paper in the paper supply section of your grocery store. Or if you only need a yard or so, you may be able to talk your local butcher or cheese shop out of a piece. Instructions for wrapping cake boards are on pages 26–27.

Food Coloring.   Paste food coloring is far superior to the liquid food coloring commonly available in your grocery store. If you don't have a gourmet supply shop or specialty bakery utensil and supply shop in your hometown, Ateco makes a whole line of paste colors obtainable by mail order. Just a dab of the paste food coloring will give you a brilliance that liquid food coloring never will. And you won't waste time mixing colors and watering down your frosting.

Scissors.   You'll need a good pair of sharp scissors for cutting countless things—cones, paper patterns, waxed freezer paper. If you get involved with tall cake sculptures, you may occasionally need a strong pair of snips to cut wooden dowels.

Metal Spatulas.   You'll probably want several lengths of metal frosting spatulas for spreading large areas of frosting. The frosting spatula I use most often has a 6-inch blade.

Matte Knife.   A matte knife (a razor-type blade with a protective covering inset into a handle) is a handy tool that will save you many cuts you might get from a single-edged razor blade when you cut to size the corrugated cardboard for your cake boards. You may not want to invest in one right away, even though it is not an expensive investment. But if you eventually do a lot of cake decorating, it will be a real hand-saver.

Knives.   You will need several slightly flexible round-tipped knives. These knives are used for spreading small areas of different-colored frostings. I prefer them to the smallest frosting spatula. Also, a sharp serrated knife will be helpful when cutting your cake shapes. An 8-inch serrated bread knife is good for sculpting cakes.

Covered Refrigerator Bowls.   One-quart plastic bowls with lids are perfect for mixing and storing small amounts of frosting. Try to find the ones that have been molded without a ridge in the bottom. Empty margarine or frozen whipped topping tubs are ideal. Just be sure to find bowls with tight-fitting lids that will keep your frosting soft while you're working. They're also great for storing leftover frosting in your refrigerator.

Paper Towels.   I don't know what I'd do without paper towels. I use them continually while I'm decorating to keep my waxed serving boards clean and to do small clean-up jobs.

Pens, Pencils, Markers.   You'll need a drawing implement of some sort for sketching your cake design and for making your paper patterns.

Toothpicks—Flat and Round.   I use flat toothpicks to help mix colors. A dab of paste color on the tip of the toothpick is often all you need to get a light color. Flat toothpicks are also used in decorating. I use them to distribute small amounts of color here and there when a decorating cone would make a line too bold. For example, when I'm working on a portrait cake, I use dabs of color on the flat toothpick to darken the area around the eyes instead of outlining the eye with a cone filled with a dark color. Toothpicks are also handy for sketching a design on a cake before you actually begin to draw with your decorating cone.

I use round toothpicks to clean out the metal tips. Round toothpicks work better than flat ones because they are stronger and pointed on both ends, though of course the flat toothpicks will work.

Either flat or round toothpicks will work for cake testing.

String. I keep a ball of easy-to-break string around and often use it as a guideline when I'm writing messages several lines long and when a line must be straight. Carefully lay the string across the cake and line it up below the area where you want to write. Move the string down as you go (see the illustration on page 22). Be sure to use lightweight string so it doesn't make a mark on your frosted cake.

Scotch Tape. You'll need transparent tape to stick the waxed freezer paper to the corrugated cardboard. You may also need it if you have to piece together waxed freezer paper to cover boards wider than the width of the paper.

MAIL-ORDER SUPPLIERS

Most department stores, hardware stores, gourmet shops, supermarkets, five-and-ten-cent stores, and specialty kitchenware shops have some or all of the necessary ingredients and supplies you'll need for your creative cakes. However, you may live in a region in which you'll need one of the following suppliers. They all have catalogs and provide mail-order service.

Maid of Scandinavia Company
3245 Raleigh Avenue
Minneapolis, MN 55416

H. Roth and Son
1577 First Avenue
New York, NY 10028

Wilton Enterprises
833 West 115 Street
Chicago, IL 60643

2

How to Do It: A Few Basic Techniques

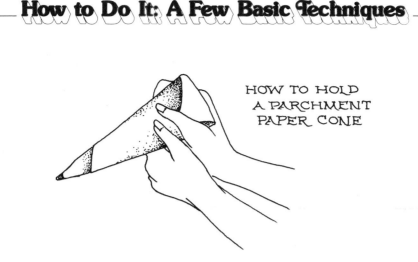

HOW TO HOLD
A PARCHMENT
PAPER CONE

Point the tip of the cone down toward the cake pan and position the tip as close as you can to the pan without their actually touching. Begin to squeeze *gently* and *steadily*. The trick is to learn to squeeze evenly, with a constant pressure. That way your lines and letters will be the same thickness. Start by drawing straight lines across the pan. Concentrate on drawing a straight line that is the same thickness all the way across the pan without breaking the line. When you're ready to end the line, don't pull up with the cone. Twist the cone quickly down toward the pan. With little effort, the frosting will break and stay in place. When you make a mistake, just wipe off the pan and start over. If you want, you can reuse the frosting by putting it back in the cone you're using or by returning it to the bowl containing the frosting you're practicing with.

After you have mastered straight, even lines, you're ready to try lettering. Begin with a clean pan. This time select an advertisement from a magazine that has words in a bold typeface, preferably one without serifs.* Using your cone again on the back of the pan, try to copy the typeface. You may want to use a lightweight string as a guideline to keep your letters in a straight line. However, it is more important now to practice forming the letters themselves. If all the letters of the alphabet are not in your ad, try to imagine what they would look like. Practice the alphabet until your letters are really clear and neat. Again, wipe the pan clean. Now practice making letters with a smaller tip, mastering each smaller size until you work your way down to a No. 1 metal tip. The No. 1 tip is perfect for very delicate lettering, fine details and outlining. It's also the most difficult to master.

Once you feel comfortable with making letters, you'll need to practice

*A serif is a fine line projecting from the main stroke of a letter.

centering them. Message layout is very important. Hyphenated words just don't make it on cakes! I find that the best way to center lettering is to cut a piece of paper the same size as your cake pan, fold it in half so that when it's unfolded the crease will serve as the center line, and sketch your lettering out in pencil on the sheet. Once you've measured your cake and placed a piece of string on its center line, the lettered sheet will serve as a general guide for centering your message on the cake. Select a brief message—"Happy Birthday" will do—and practice centering it on any handy cake pan. Eventually you'll develop an eye for centering, and laying out your message won't be necessary unless it's lengthy.

If you find that even after lots of practice you can't master perfect lettering, you can still put messages on your cakes by using a free-style print. Just use a lightweight string as your guideline so your letters will follow a straight line. Lay the string across your pan, and after you finish the line, move it down the pan.

LETTERING WITH A STRING

STRING   CAKEPAN

One last tip: When you're drawing with a decorating cone on a frosted cake, it's sometimes helpful to draw your lines lightly with a toothpick on the frosting first. This will serve as a guide when you use your decorating cone. And if you make a mistake, you can simply smooth out the frosting and start again.

MIXING COLORS

Mixing colors is one of the most important activities in creative cake art. Bright, clear, realistic colors can make the difference between a good attempt and a smashing success. And if you're matching a design, careful color mixing is essential. One time I made cakes in the shapes of the complete line of Church and Dwight's Arm & Hammer products for a celebration of a banner sales year. Had I substituted for their identifiable yellow, red and blue logo, pale yellow, pink and turquoise, they wouldn't have been satisfied.

As I mentioned earlier, I use paste food coloring in my frosting. Paste food coloring comes in a broad range of colors and can be purchased at gourmet supply stores or bakery suppliers or by mail order (see p. 12). I use Ateco brand colors, though Maid of Scandinavia and Wilton also make them. Paste food coloring gives more brilliant results than liquid food coloring, and it doesn't water down your frosting.

Paste food coloring should be stored at room temperature. It will last indefinitely if kept tightly sealed. If a jar has been stored for a long time, the paste may separate somewhat. Simply stir until the paste is mixed and it will be good as new. There is never any reason to add water to paste colors.

When coloring a batch of frosting, always remember to color slightly more than you think you'll need. I learned the hard way that *you can seldom match colors*. You can't "stretch" frosting. If you don't have enough frosting to color the required area of your cake and you must mix more, it's likely that the new frosting will dry a different shade. In most cases, it will ruin the look of your cake. Also, remember that the colors always set slightly darker or brighter than they look when you mix them.

Don't worry about waste when making a generous amount of every color of frosting. Leftover frosting will keep at least two weeks when put in a tightly sealed bowl in the refrigerator. What's more, kids love buttercream frosting on graham crackers. You can make them a special after-school treat and practice your lettering by personalizing every cracker.

I have no established order or method for mixing colors. Sometimes I mix all the colors I need for a special cake before I begin working on it, and other times I mix them as I go. It really doesn't matter. It just depends on how eager you are to get started. You'll find one method that works best for you.

When you're ready to color your frosting, use a bowl only slightly larger than the amount of frosting you want. That way it's easier to utilize all the food coloring that collects on the sides of the bowl. Always use clean utensils to mix the food coloring into the frosting. If your spoon or knife has frosting of another color on it, it will distort the color you're mixing. Also, if your knife is coated with frosting that has begun to harden and crystallize, those crystals will ruin your new batch of frosting: lumpy frosting won't spread smoothly and will clog the metal tips of your decorating cones.

When you're preparing to color a large portion of frosting, never add paste food coloring directly to the entire mixture. If you add a big blob of food coloring all at once to a batch of frosting, chances are that the food coloring will never dissolve and your frosting will be filled with tiny dots of food coloring that will cause streaking. To avoid this, measure out about ½ cup of frosting in a small bowl and thoroughly mix in ½ teaspoon of food coloring. Then put the colored frosting back in the bowl containing the large batch of frosting, and mix well. Repeat this procedure until the entire mixture is the desired color.

When you're coloring a cup or less of frosting, start by adding a toothpick tip measure of paste color. Mix with a spoon or rubber spatula. Continue to add toothpick tips of color, mixing after every addition, until the color is right. Don't forget: The color will continue to brighten for the next ten or fifteen minutes, and will finally set somewhat brighter still.

Here's a basic lesson in color mixing: The primary colors are red, yellow and blue. The secondary colors are green, purple and orange. You'll achieve green by mixing equal parts of yellow and blue. You'll get yellow-green by adding more yellow than green. And you'll get blue-green by adding more blue than yellow. The same applies when you mix red and yellow to make orange, and red and blue to make purple. Red and green make brown. All colors combined will give you a dark muddy gray-brown. The muddy color is not very appetizing, but you may use it to make black frosting for outline and detail.

The best method when coloring frosting is to experiment with a little color at a time. Eventually you'll learn how much color it will take to give you the tint or shade you desire. As with every other aspect of cake decorating, it simply takes practice.

Ordinarily, I don't mix frostings of two different colors together to get a third color. Paste food coloring comes in such a broad range of colors that it isn't necessary. And of course time can be saved by stocking a large collection of colors. However, to prevent considerable waste when only a small amount of a specific color is needed, adding frosting of one color to a batch of another color can be more economical. When you're decorating a cake that requires many colors, this method of mixing can seem complicated at first. But if you carefully list all the colors you're going to need, and the approximate amounts necessary, you'll soon be able to figure out the color breakdowns very easily.

To color your frosting economically and efficiently, you need to think ahead. Figure out approximately how much frosting you'll need of each color. It may be helpful at first to draw a sketch of your cake, label the colors, and then make a list of what colors you'll need in what quantities. Eventually you'll learn to mix and reuse your colors to make other colors and thereby save time and frosting.

Necktie cake

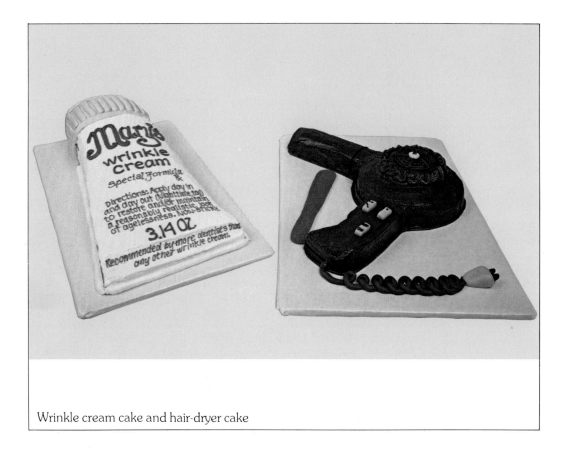

Wrinkle cream cake and hair-dryer cake

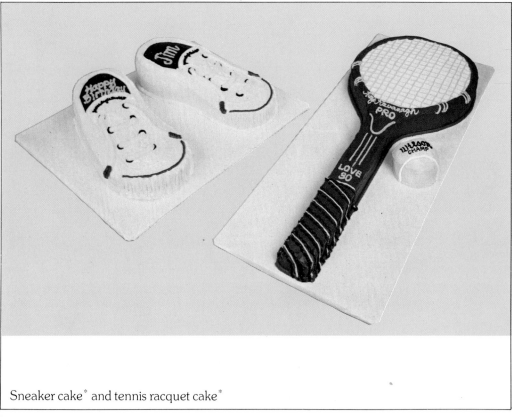

Sneaker cake* and tennis racquet cake*

*Instructions for starred cakes appear in the text.

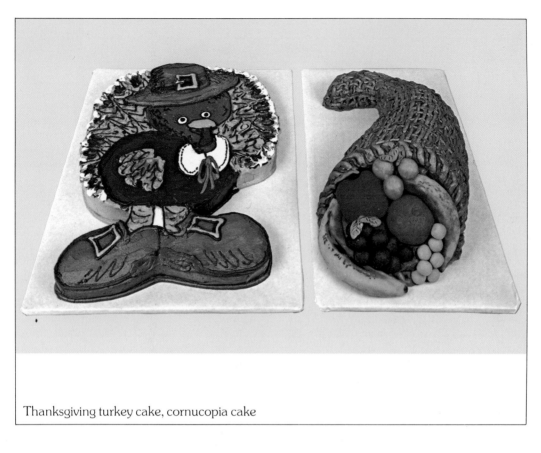

Thanksgiving turkey cake, cornucopia cake

Christmas stocking cake, Christmas tree cake,* and holiday umbrella cake

Typewriter cake[*]

Clown cake[*] and hamburger cake[*]

Telephone cake, pencil cake and message cake

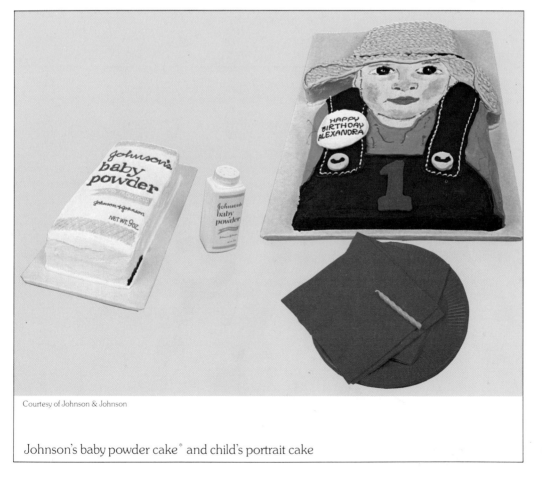

Johnson's baby powder cake* and child's portrait cake

Paddington Bear cake

Car cake and airplane cake

Spring bonnet cake*

Mini creative cakes*: "cheesecake" and slice-of-cake cake

Bottle of scotch cake

SPREADING FROSTING SMOOTHLY

In order to make fine and detailed illustrations on creative cakes, it's necessary to frost your cake as smoothly as possible. Delicate design simply won't work on a rough surface. The greatest impediment to smooth frosting is crumbs, which can lift off the surface of the cake and mix with the frosting to create a rough and dimpled surface. So the main trick to smooth frosting is avoiding crumbs.

Before you even begin to frost, remember that the surface texture of the cake is important: if the cake is moist, your frosting will spread smoothly, but if the cake is dry, you're likely to have trouble with crumbs. If you're frosting a dry cake, proceed with extra caution.

To begin frosting, drop several tablespoonfuls of frosting near the edges on the top of your cake. Now take a frosting spatula that fits comfortably in your hand. The one I prefer is about four inches long. If the cake is a cutout shape to be frosted with only one color, it's easier to frost the sides first, then work on the top. However, if your design is such that several sections of the cake are different colors, begin on the top and work down over the sides. Whichever way you start, use a light touch and begin spreading the frosting over a small area of your cake. Pick up more frosting on your spatula as you need it and continue working, extending the area you've just frosted. Smooth out stroke marks as you go along. If you allow the frosting to set too long without smoothing away the stroke marks, they'll harden and become difficult to erase. Work quickly on a small area at a time. Be careful not to pull up the upper crust of your cake when you lift your spatula from the surface. If you do pull it up, you'll have a tough time getting rid of crumbs. Dunk your spatula in tepid water from time to time. A slightly moistened spatula won't be as apt to stick to the frosting and pull it up with crumbs. The moisture also helps to smooth the surface of the frosting. Occasionally dunking your spatula in water also keeps it from getting coated with crystallized frosting. A spatula with crystallized frosting will leave streak marks in the frosting you are trying to smooth. But don't use too much water or your frosting will become sticky with little pools on the surface.

Once you have frosted the top of your cake, you are ready to tackle the sides. Because many creative cakes are sculpted and cut into shapes, you will often be frosting raw edges. Frosting raw edges demands the same technique as spreading frosting smoothly, but you must be especially careful to avoid crumbs. When you have a raw, uncrusted edge of a cake to frost, take a spatula full of frosting and gently dab it on the side of the cake. Make another dab of frosting a few inches away and continue until you have four or five dabs of frosting in close proximity. Moisten your spatula and carefully spread one dab until it joins another. Repeat, joining frosting to frosting as you go around the sides of your cake and moistening your spatula regularly.

People often ask me if I glaze the raw edges of my cakes before icing them. When the glaze sets, it creates a kind of seal that helps to keep your subsequent frosting free of crumbs. I've never used this method, but if you have trouble with the crumbs when you frost raw edges you might want to experiment with glazing the edges first. You simply take about half a cup of frosting and add water until the mixture is the consistency of a very thick cream. Apply this mixture to the raw surface of your cake. Allow it to dry thoroughly, then frost with your regular frosting.

MAKING A SERVING BOARD

For every cake you decorate, you will need to make a serving board by covering a piece of corrugated cardboard with waxed white freezer paper. I always use white freezer paper because it sets off cake colors very nicely and

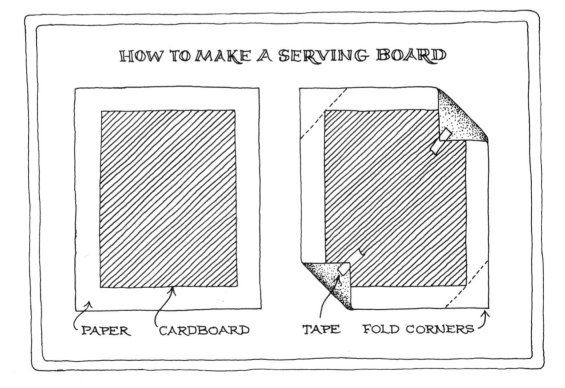

HOW TO MAKE A SERVING BOARD

PAPER   CARDBOARD   TAPE   FOLD CORNERS

the frosting isn't absorbed by the waxed paper. For an 11 × 17-inch cake, you'll need a 14 × 18-inch piece of cardboard, and a piece of freezer paper 4 inches wider and longer than your board. I always allow at least 2 inches to fold under each side. To cover the board, place the freezer paper on a table, waxed side down. Now place your cardboard on the paper, centering it in the middle. Fold the corners of the paper over the corners of the cardboard. Tape each paper corner to the cardboard. Now fold the sides under and tape securely, working top to bottom, side to side. You now have a serving board.

MAKING PAPER PATTERNS

The fun of Creative Cakes is that every cake is a new and different one. And even if the cake is a repeat—Mickey Mouse and Snoopy are frequent requests—I design it differently every time. So one time Snoopy might be holding Woodstock, and another he could be wearing a big yellow straw hat. Every cake is designed specifically for every new order.

My endlessly different designs are possible because I never use form pans or molds. Instead, I use paper patterns to make my unusual shapes. It might be easier to make Mickey Mouse from a form pan, but how many times will Mickey Mouse fit your occasion? The form pan that may seem economical because there is no cake waste becomes an expensive investment when you only use it once or twice.

Paper patterns also allow great freedom of expression. You can create practically any cake you can draw. Once you've mastered the basic techniques of pattern-making, you'll find most any idea can become a creative cake.

In the beginning, it probably will be easier and more economical for you to follow the patterns in this book fairly exactly. But once you feel comfortable making and using cake patterns, you'll want to try variations of my suggested cakes, and eventually you'll want to create original cakes using your own ideas.

One last word on making paper patterns for your cakes: you can't always design cakes that will require every bit of the sheet cake you baked. It may not seem economical for you to waste cake, and you'll probably want patterns that use up as much cake as possible. Unfortunately I find that whenever I try to design that way, the cakes seem stilted. They don't have the "artsy" flow and technique that I think my own patterns should have. To my mind, allowing for a little waste may not be as money-wise, but it certainly gives you more freedom for creativity. You'll have to work out your own priorities on this. In any event, you are bound to wind up with cake scraps. I always have plenty of scraps around. They serve as samples for prospective customers. But scraps can be creative, too, as you'll see later in the section on mini creative cakes (p. 113). Making a paper pattern is really a fairly simple procedure. First you need to decide what size cake to make. This will be determined by the number of people to be served. I generally work from an 11 × 17-inch sheet cake, which will serve thirty people. Prepare your cake, and while it's still in the oven, you can make a serving board (see the preceding section). For an 11 × 17-inch flat cake, you'll need an 18 × 14-inch serving board. (If your pattern is a really unusual shape, you may want to draw your pattern first and then cut the board to fit.)

After your board is covered, cut another piece of freezer paper the same size as your board from which to make your pattern. Lay it waxed side down on top of your serving board. If you are not very artistic, you may want to use graph paper for your pattern.

You're now ready to make your pattern, so take a pencil in hand. Draw the parts of your cake on your pattern paper. Remember that many creative cakes are comprised of one main pattern for the large part of the cake plus several small patterns for additional features. After you've drawn your pattern, cut it out with your scissors. Cool your cake in the pan for at least one hour. Then lay the paper pattern on top of the cake while it is still in the pan. Cut around the paper pattern with a sharp knife. Now take another wax-covered board (not your serving board) and place it on top of the cake. Flip the cake upside down. Pull away the parchment paper you used to line your cake pan. Then pull away the cake pieces that are not part of your pattern or pieces that need to be assembled with the main cake. (Save the cake scraps.) Take the serving board, rest it on top of the cake, waxed side to the cake, and flip the cake upright. Now attach any additional pieces, using frosting as mortar, and continue with your decorating.

BASIC DECORATING STEPS

Here is a start-to-finish rundown of the basic procedure you'll use with *every* cake.

1. Bake the cake and cool it for at least one hour.
2. Cover a serving board that is the appropriate size for your cake.
3. Mix your frosting and store it in a bowl with a fitted lid or a bowl covered with a damp towel to prevent crystals from forming on the frosting.
4. Draw and cut out your paper pattern for your creative cake (see preceding section).

5. Place the pattern pieces on the cake while it is still in the pan, and cut with a knife around the edges until all your cake pieces are cut out.

6. Remove the scraps and arrange your cake pieces on your serving board, brushing crumbs off the board when you're finished.

7. Determine what colors in what amounts you will need for your design and mix them in separate bowls. It may be helpful to draw a rough sketch of what your finished cake will look like and indicate every color on the sketch.

8. Make and fill a parchment cone (or a nylon one) for every color that you'll be using.

9. Frost your cake, being careful to smooth the surface with a knife dipped occasionally in a bowl of water. Avoid using too much water: it can create tiny pools on top of your cake.

10. Sketch the designs that you want to draw on your cake with a toothpick and then fill in the lines with appropriate colors. Try not to "layer" too much frosting: it can make a serving piece of cake too sweet.

11. Caulk around the bottom of the cake to preserve freshness and to make the edge look finished, clean and neat.

THREE-DIMENSIONAL CAKES

Sculptured, three-dimensional cakes are truly the most fun to make. They are one giant step away from flat cakes, and they allow you to be wildly imaginative with your cake art. They also demand more time, ingenuity and cake. I suggest that you move slowly at first with sculptured cakes: make a few simple ones first and master the basic techniques before you plunge into a complicated three-dimensional cake.

Sculptured cakes require a slightly more complicated design process because you must visualize the cake in all its component parts before you can even make the pattern. If you've ever sculpted anything from clay or mud or even sand, you're already ahead of the game because you'll have had some experience visualizing a three-dimensional structure and then putting it together.

As you become more experienced with cake sculpture, you'll be able to add and subtract bits of cake from your final product without much trouble. But because cake crumbles and falls apart, you'll find that the more carefully you make your patterns and cut your cake parts, the more successful your sculpted cake will be.

The main challenge with sculptured cakes is pattern-making. Envisioning the pattern for a sculpted cake is more difficult than for a flat cake because you must visualize more than just the outline of the cake: you must make a separate pattern for every layer of your sculpture.

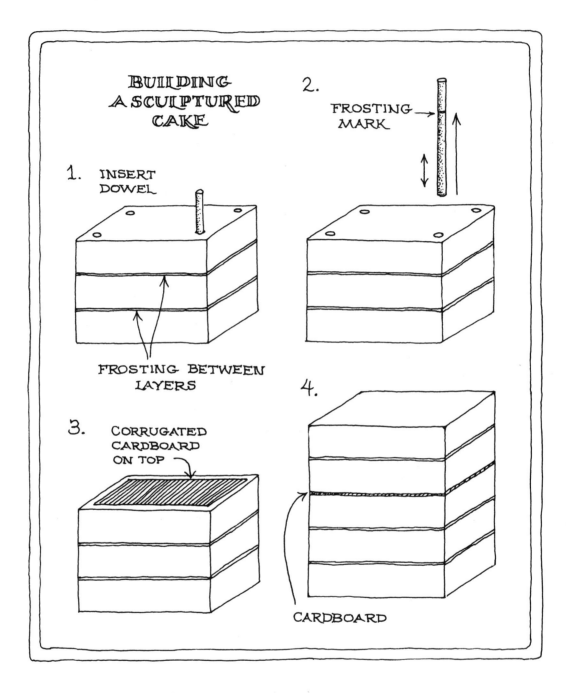

BUILDING
A SCULPTURED
CAKE

2. FROSTING
MARK

1. INSERT
DOWEL

FROSTING BETWEEN
LAYERS

3. CORRUGATED
CARDBOARD
ON TOP

4.

CARDBOARD

If the cake is a simple shape, such as a book or a bottle, the pattern-making is easy: if the cake is going to be two layers high you simple cut one pattern and then cut two pieces from the same pattern and layer them. But if the cake is a more complicated shape—for example, a pair of sneakers—then you must think of each layer as a separate pattern. With a sneaker, you need to cut one pattern for the base of the shoe and another, about half the size of the first, for the top part of the shoe where the laces are.

The best way to envision a sculpted cake in its necessary parts is to do a side-view sketch of the cake. Once you have a clear outline of what the cake will look like from the side, you can break it down into parts, or layers, for pattern-making.

You'll find it helpful to study the sculptured cakes I've given instructions for, such as the watermelon cake, the sneakers (p. 62), and the spring bonnet (p. 75). These instructions will give you a better sense of how to break a sculptured cake down into parts and layers.

The most important sculpting technique for the three-dimensional cakes is the use of frosting as mortar. All sculpted cakes, even ones as simple as a strawberry or a slice of watermelon, need the additional strength of frosting between every layer. Naturally, the color of the frosting doesn't matter, but I normally use uncolored buttercream or chocolate frosting because I prefer all the frosting between the layers to look the same when the cake is cut and the frosting revealed. However, if it doesn't matter to you, you can use up some of your leftover frosting that you've kept tightly covered in the refrigerator.

There are times when the frosting mortar simply isn't strong enough to support your cake. If a cake is more than four layers high, for example, you will usually need additional reinforcements so that the cake will stand straight and the frosting won't ooze out between the layers from the weight of the cake.

The best way to reinforce a sculpted cake is with wooden dowels (available at any lumber yard) and corrugated cardboard. Here's all you do: When you're building a cake sculpture and you have four layers with frosting spread between each one and you must make the sculpture still higher, cut a sheet of corrugated cardboard the same size as the uppermost layer. Now lightly frost the top layer.

1. Take your wooden dowel (¼ or ⅜ inch) and stick it down through all four layers of cake.

2. Next, carefully pull out the dowel and notice where the frosting left its mark on the dowel. The mark will indicate the length you want to make your dowels. I usually cut four dowels, one for each corner. But if the cake is especially large, you'll want to put additional dowels along the edges and in

the center of your cake. Cut the dowel at the frosting mark with a saw, a strong pair of scissors or a very sharp knife. Be sure all dowels are exactly the same length. If your cake is slightly uneven, the dowels will even it out for you.

After you have four dowels cut exactly the same size, stick one in each corner. Dab extra frosting around each dowel and in the center of the cake.

3. Now rest the cardboard on the top of your top layer and continue to build your sculpture, remembering to frost between the layers.

Once you've mastered pattern-making and cake reinforcement, you're ready to make most any sculpted cake. The only other factors to keep in mind are the increased possibility of frosting slipping down the sides of a very high cake—just be sure not to put it on too thick or add too many candy decorations—and the difficulty of transporting sculptured cakes—you're not going to want to carry an Empire State Building cake across town!

CANDY DECORATIONS

Much of the fun I have with my cakes comes when I use molded marzipan (see p. 51) and other candies to add another dimension to them. A cake in the shape of a push-button telephone is much more interesting when the buttons actually protrude from the cake. Typewriter keys, car wheels, and sometimes tiny people are made from marzipan on my cakes.

For example, one time I had an order for a service-station cake. A five-year-old named Austin loved cars and trucks. The base or drive-in area of the station was a 12-inch square sheet cake frosted with white buttercream. On top, centered and toward the back, was a 4-inch square double layer cake that was also frosted with white frosting. That 4-inch square was the service station. I used decorating cones filled with black and red frosting to draw windows, doors and garage doors—even the ladies' and men's room doors—on "Austin's Service Station."

But the real fun began when I was ready to make the cars, tow truck and gas pumps. The cars and truck were all molded from colored marzipan. I rolled black marzipan into tiny circles to make a pile of inner tubes. Colored Tootsie Rolls were used for gas pumps. And I even made a signboard for the price of gas. I rolled a yellow Tootsie Roll out with a rolling pin to flatten it. I then cut it into a 2 × ½-inch rectangle and folded it in half lengthwise to make a sandwich board. I then used a cone with a No. 1 tip to write the price of gas on the board. That piece was placed in front of the station. When you allow yourself, your imagination will run wild and you'll come up with all sorts of details.

When you make marzipan, it will be an off-white color. When wrapped tightly in Saran Wrap and placed in an airtight plastic container (Tupperware is terrific), it will keep for a long time. If you don't want to make it yourself, marzipan comes in 10-ounce rolls and may be purchased in most supermarkets and gourmet shops. Marzipan is usually stocked in the section where imported delicacies are sold in the supermarket.

Tootsie Rolls, gumdrops, jelly beans, Life Savers, licorice laces and sticks, spearmint leaves and frosted pretzel logs can add dimension and also be decorative additions to your cakes. You'll find them in most candy departments. I recommend staying away from colored sugars, chocolate Jimmies and other prepared bakery supplies because they really don't taste very good.

FREEZING AND STORING CAKES

Freezing cakes is a handy way to save scraps until you're ready to use them. Or if you must work way ahead of schedule, you may want to freeze a decorated cake. Generally, a frozen cake should stay fresh for about four months, but I wouldn't recommend freezing cake for more than a month. The longer the cake has been frozen, the quicker it seems to dry out when it is subsequently cut. In other words, while a freshly baked and decorated cake may stay moist and delicious for several days—even a week—after it's been cut, a cake that's been frozen often loses its freshness after the first day. Nonetheless, there will be times when making the cake ahead and freezing it is the only way you'll be able to fit a creative cake into your schedule.

Freezing procedure depends on whether or not the cake is frosted. To freeze unfrosted cake or cake scraps, be sure the cakes have cooled thoroughly. Then place the cake on a covered serving board and cover with aluminum foil or plastic wrap. Make the package as airtight as possible. Then place the wrapped cake inside a large plastic bag and again seal tightly with a wire twist. Freeze.

If you plan to freeze more than one unfrosted sheet cake or several cake layers, you may want to stack the cakes to save space in your freezer. If so, when you remove the cake from its cake pan, leave the parchment liner on your cake to keep it from sticking to the next cake in the stack. Of course you can always put waxed paper between the layers. And avoid stacking more than three layers together. Once you've stacked your cakes, double-wrap as previously instructed.

When you're ready to defrost your cake, remove it from the freezer, take it out of the plastic bag—leaving it wrapped in foil—and allow the cake to thaw for a couple of hours. Now unwrap the aluminum foil and place the cake on a serving board. Be certain the condensation on the surface has evaporated before you begin frosting. You may want to gently blot it with an absorbent paper towel. Frosting won't stick to a very moist surface.

If you're going to freeze one of your decorated masterpieces, *be careful.* I seldom freeze my finished works of art because I don't want to risk having the design ruined by possible freezer burn or accidental crushing. However, many times I make scraps into decorated mini-cakes, and I always freeze them. If you go by the following directions, you should have no problem.

Place your decorated cake and serving board in a box. Be sure there is plenty of room between the top of the cake and the top of the box. Tape the box closed. Now place the entire box inside a large plastic bag. You may have to use a wastebasket liner bag. Seal the bag with the twist provided. Freeze your cake.

Remove the cake from the freezer the day before you plan to serve it. *Immediately* take it out of the plastic bag. Now put it back into the *refrigerator,* box and all. Several hours before you serve your cake, place it in a *cool place.* This will prevent heat extremes that can cause melting of the buttercream frosting. Buttercream gets wet and drippy if it is exposed to heat or humidity too quickly.

If possible, try to avoid freezing cakes for summertime parties. You never know how hot or humid it's going to be on the day of your party. And as I mentioned, the heat is merciless on frozen buttercream frosting. If you must freeze, though—and many of my customers do it every year when I take my summer vacation—bring the cake to room temperature near an air conditioner. Naturally, the above applies to those of you who live in warm climates all year long.

Special Note: You don't need to refrigerate any cake you decorate with buttercream frosting. Simply placing it in a tightly sealed box or under a cake dome will keep it fresh for a couple of days. However, if you do refrigerate it, remember not to expose your cake to heat extremes too quickly.

And while I'm on the subject of heat extremes, you may find your frosting drippy and uncooperative if you decide to decorate on a particularly hot and/or humid day. If your kitchen is not air-conditioned, don't try to work on such a day. Your frosting will take two or three times as long to set—if it sets at all. And often you'll be dissatisfied with your results.

SOME HANDY TABLES

Measuring Batter

A normal recipe for a cake calling for two regular 8- or 9-inch round pans usually yields between 5 and 6 cups of batter.

Always measure your oven before investing in cake pans. Allow 1½ inches of extra room on all sides of your pan.

The following list gives cake pan sizes and the amount of batter needed to fill each one. Remember, too little or too much batter in a cake pan may cause any number of cake failures. These pans are all sheet cake or layer cake pans from 1 inch to 1½ inches deep.

6-inch round—1½ cups batter
8-inch round—2¼ cups batter
9-inch round—2½ cups batter
10-inch round—3½ cups batter
12-inch round—5¾ cups batter
14-inch round—8 cups batter
18-inch round—12 cups batter
8-inch square—3½ cups batter
9 × 13-inch sheet cake—5 cups batter
10 × 14-inch sheet cake—6 cups batter
11 × 17-inch sheet cake—8 cups batter
18 × 26-inch sheet cake—16 cups batter

Note: If you have an irregular-sized pan and want to figure out how much batter it takes to fill it sufficiently, fill the pan with water. Measure the water. Now figure two-thirds the water capacity. That gives you the amount of batter you need for the pan.

TABLE OF WEIGHTS AND MEASURES
(Common U.S. Measures and Metric System)

1 teaspoon = $\frac{1}{16}$ ounce = 5 milliliters
3 teaspoons = 1 tablespoon = ½ ounce = 15 milliliters
16 tablespoons = 1 cup = 8 fluid ounces
1 ounce = 28.35 grams
3½ ounces = 100 grams
0.035 ounces = 1 gram
8 ounces = 250 grams
1 cup = ½ pint
2 cups = 1 pint
4 cups = 2 pints = 1 quart
4⅓ cups = 1 quart 2 ounces (1.056 quarts) = 1 liter or 1000 milliliters
1 cup plus ¼ tablespoon = 8 ounces = ¼ liter
4 quarts = 1 gallon
1 quart = 946.4 milliliters
1.06 quarts = 1 liter

TABLE OF EQUIVALENTS

1 stick butter or margarine = ½ cup
4 sticks butter or margarine = 1 pound
2½ cups shortening = 1 pound
2 cups sugar = 1 pound
2½ cups brown sugar = 1 pound
3½–4 cups confectioners' sugar = 1 pound
1 medium-sized egg = 2 ounces
1 cup chopped nuts = ¼ pound
4 cups all-purpose flour (sifted or stirred) = 1 pound
4½ cups cake flour (sifted or stirred) = 1 pound

SUBSTITUTION TABLE

1 cup cake flour = 1 cup minus 2 tablespoons all-purpose flour
1 cup milk = ½ cup evaporated milk plus ½ cup water
1 cup sour milk or buttermilk = 1 tablespoon lemon juice or vinegar plus milk to make 1 cup
    (Allow to stand 5 minutes.)
1 square (1 ounce) unsweetened chocolate = 3 tablespoons cocoa powder plus 1 tablespoon
    butter or margarine
¼ teaspoon baking soda plus ½ teaspoon cream of tartar = 1 teaspoon baking powder
1 tablespoon cornstarch = 2 tablespoons flour
1 tablespoon vinegar plus 1 cup evaporated milk = 1 cup sour cream

3
Recipes

CAKES

It has always been my belief that creative cakes are most successful when the cakes are made from basic recipes with fresh ingredients. And of course all my recipes are made from scratch. I just don't believe that cakes made from mixes can ever compare to the home-made variety. My success is based on a good ole chocolate-cake recipe that my mother used for every birthday cake I ever had. Today it's the only cake I sell. When I first opened my Creative Cakes business, in addition to my basic chocolate cake, I offered a plain butter cake, a peanut cake and a chocolate chip cake. But once the word of my chocolate cake got out, the requests for the others became fewer and fewer. Eventually, I eliminated all other recipes. It seems most everybody loves chocolate cake. As an extra bonus, making only chocolate cakes saves me considerable time and storage space. If you have a recipe that always gets rave reviews and goes well with buttercream frosting, I'd stick with it. If you don't, perhaps you'll find a favorite among the recipes that follow.

The recipes I've included here are ones that have been used by my family and friends and passed on to me. My personal favorite is the peanut cake made from freshly ground peanuts. It involves a little more work than most of the cake recipes here, but if you're a peanut freak as I am, every bite makes the extra work worthwhile. Whenever I make a peanut cake for a friend—as I said earlier, I make only chocolate cakes for business—I always flavor the frosting with orange extract. It's really a special treat. Fancy baking is not my specialty. I prefer the basic cakes that you'll find in this chapter.

I've often heard people say that if you can read, you can bake. I've got to go along with that theory to some degree; however, cake baking is one type of baking that requires accuracy. A little of this and a little of that can cause any number of cake failures. Your oven temperature, measurements, length and speed of mixing, and timing must be accurate. For example, if your oven is too hot, your cake may shrink in the pan or crack on top. If, on the other hand, the temperature is too low, your cake may fall in the middle or become dry from overbaking.

Remember that you must preheat your oven. Usually ten minutes is long enough. If you are uncertain about how accurate the thermostat on your oven is, buy an oven thermometer and check the oven temperature. Adjust the thermostat on your oven accordingly. For example, if your oven thermostat is set at 350°F., but your oven thermometer reads 325°, remember that your oven is about 25° off.

Make sure your oven racks are level; if they aren't, your cakes will be lopsided. Once you place your cake in the preheated oven, do not move it. If you do, chances are your cake will fall. Since heat rises, the best place to place your cake for baking is on the center rack. If more than one pan is in the oven at the same time, never allow the two pans to touch. Leave at least one and a half inches around each pan. It's important for air to be able to circulate all around every pan.

If your measurements aren't accurate—for example, you put in too little sugar or too much baking powder or soda—the texture of your cake may be coarse. If you add too much flour, your cake will be dry. If you don't use enough baking powder or baking soda, your cake won't rise. If there are cracks in your cake, you may have added too much flour. Not enough shortening or sugar will cause toughness. And if the top crust on your cake is sticky and moist, you may have used too much liquid or sugar.

Mixing is as important as measuring ingredients. Be certain to scrape the sides of the bowl and the beaters during mixing. Also, do not overmix. If you use an electric mixer, one minute at a low speed once the flour has been added is enough time to blend. Scrape the sides of the bowl. Then mix well for no more than another two minutes at a medium speed, continually scraping the sides of your bowl. Overmixing may cause cracks or a cake that won't rise.

Finally, your cake must bake just the right length of time. If you take your cake from the oven before it's finished baking, it will fall and be gooey in the middle. If you allow it to bake too long, it will dry out, shrink in the pan and crack on top.

Cakes often take longer to bake than the time specified in the recipe. Even if you're using the same recipe, the baking time for your cake may vary from one time to the next. If a baking time is given, check your cake after the shortest prescribed time. Always check it with a cake tester. You may use a metal cake tester, a toothpick (what I use) or even a broom straw, if you have nothing else. (I'll assume you have the good sense to clean it!) I don't trust the touch-the-center-of-the-cake-to-see-if-it-springs-back method of testing. The cake-tester method is much safer. If the cake tester comes out clean when you insert it in the center of the cake, the cake's done. Easy as that. When testing a large sheet cake, I take no chances—I test the cake in several places.

Always let your cakes cool completely before you frost them. I never attempt to begin frosting until the cake has cooled at least one hour. Also, remember to cool cakes on a cooling rack.

I hope these hints have been helpful. If you are really concerned about failures you've had in your baking, perhaps you should go to your library and check out some cookbooks on baking for more information. With all this in mind, enjoy the following recipes.

Aunt Frannie's Crazy Cake

This is a terrific chocolate cake that has been in my family for over a hundred years. My Aunt Frannie claims my great-grandmother taught it to her when she was five years old. However, I'll attribute this recipe to my Aunt Frannie because she's the one who first gave it to me. The reason she calls it crazy is because you simply put all but one of the ingredients into a bowl at once, and when the last ingredient is added—the boiling water—you mix it all up. Easy as that. And it bakes into a rich, moist, truly tasty treat for chocolate lovers.

Preheat oven to 325°F.
Line a 9 × 13-inch sheet cake pan *or* two 8-inch square pans with parchment paper.

2 cups sugar	1 teaspoon salt
2 eggs	2 teaspoons baking powder
1 cup milk	1 teaspoon baking soda
1 cup cocoa	2 teaspoons vanilla extract
1 cup shortening	3 cups all-purpose flour
(I use Crisco)	1 cup boiling water

In a large mixing bowl put all the ingredients except the water in the order in which they are listed. *Do not stir.* Add boiling water last and then mix well. Pour batter into the prelined pan and bake for 30 minutes, or until a cake tester inserted in the center of the cake comes out clean. Cool at least one hour before frosting.

Candy Lou's Champion 4-H Butter Cake

My cousin Candy Lou brought home many blue ribbons during her years of participation in 4-H. However, the one she most prized was the Grand Champion Award she received at the Indiana state fair for her butter cake.

Preheat oven to 375°F.
Line a 9 × 13-inch sheet cake pan with parchment paper.

2½ cups sifted cake flour	½ cup soft butter
1½ cups sugar	1 cup milk
3 teaspoons baking powder	1½ teaspoons vanilla extract
1 teaspoon salt	2 eggs

Sift flour into the large bowl of an electric mixer. Then sift sugar, baking powder and salt into the bowl. Add butter and pour in ½ cup of the milk. Add vanilla. Beat ½ minute on low speed to moisten flour. Add another ¼ cup milk, then beat for two minutes on medium speed, scraping bowl as necessary. Add eggs and the remaining ¼ cup of milk. Beat another 1½ minutes at medium speed. Do not overbeat. Pour into pan. Bake 25 to 30 minutes, or until a cake tester inserted in the center of the cake comes out clean. Cool at least one hour before decorating.

White Cake

In my opinion, white cakes are somewhat boring. It seems to me that if you're going to indulge in cake calories, it should be for a rich and delicious peanut butter or chocolate cake. Nonetheless, you may have occasions for a white cake. The best recipe I've ever found is in the *Betty Crocker Cook Book*. It's called Rich Silver Cake.

The following recipe also works well as a sheet cake, which is what you'll want for your creative cakes.

Preheat oven to 350°F.
Line a 17 × 11-inch sheet cake pan with parchment paper.

¾ cup shortening	½ teaspoon salt
1½ cups sugar	4 teaspoons baking powder
1 teaspoon vanilla extract	1 cup milk
½ teaspoon almond extract	4 egg whites
2¾ cups sifted cake flour	

In the large bowl of a mixer, cream shortening until light. Gradually add 1 cup of the sugar, beating well after each addition. Continue beating until the mixture is light and fluffy. Add vanilla and almond extract. Into a separate bowl, sift flour with salt and baking powder. Add dry ingredients and milk alternately to sugar and shortening mixture, and blend well after each addition. In a medium-sized mixing bowl, beat egg whites until stiff. Add the remaining ½ cup of sugar gradually to the egg whites, and continue beating until the mixture is stiff and shiny. Carefully fold egg whites into the rest of the batter.

Pour batter into the pan and spread it out evenly in the pan with a rubber spatula. Bake 25 to 30 minutes, or until a cake tester inserted in the center of the cake comes out clean. Cool at least an hour before decorating.

Peanut Banana Cake

If you're one of those peanut butter-and-banana sandwich lovers, here's your cake! It's moist and delicious and direct from the Peanut Growers of America.

Preheat oven to 350°F.
Line an 11 × 17-inch sheet cake pan with parchment paper.

1 cup butter or margarine	5 cups all-purpose flour
2 cups sugar	5 teaspoons baking powder
4 eggs	1 teaspoon salt
1½ cups milk	1½ cups finely chopped peanuts
2 cups mashed ripe bananas	

In a large bowl, cream butter or margarine and sugar until light and fluffy. Beat in eggs. Stir in milk and bananas. In another bowl, sift together flour, baking powder, and salt. Stir peanuts into dry ingredients. Add dry ingredients to cake batter, and beat until smooth and well-blended. Do not overbeat. Pour into cake pan. Bake 30 to 35 minutes, or until cake tester inserted in the center of the cake comes out clean. Do not attempt to decorate for at least an hour after it's cooled.

Peanut-Butter Fudge Cake

This is a great cake for a peanut butter/chocolate freak—the person who craves Reese's peanut-butter cups. It's great with peanut-butter frosting. And if you're making a cake to look like a jar of Skippy peanut butter, it's a natural.

Preheat oven to 350°F.
Line a 9 × 13-inch sheet cake pan with parchment paper.

¾ cup butter or margarine	chocolate, melted in a dou-
1 cup peanut butter*	ble boiler
2¼ cups sugar	3 cups sifted cake flour
1½ teaspoons vanilla extract	1½ teaspoons baking soda
3 eggs	¾ teaspoon salt
3 1-ounce squares unsweetened	1½ cups ice water

*I like to use the crunchy kind, but smooth peanut butter works all right.

In a large bowl, cream butter or margarine, peanut butter, sugar and vanilla. Add eggs. Beat this mixture until it's fluffy. Add melted chocolate and blend well. In another bowl, sift together dry ingredients. Add alternately with water to peanut butter-chocolate mixture. Pour into prepared cake pan. Bake for 30 to 35 minutes, or until a cake tester inserted in the center of the cake comes out clean. Cool at least an hour before frosting.

Peanut Cake

Here's my favorite cake. It will stay moist and delicious for a week if you have it around that long. It has a delicate peanutty flavor rather than a peanut-butter taste because it uses freshly ground peanuts instead of peanut butter. I prefer Spanish peanuts with the skins left on, but any roasted peanut will do. Grinding peanuts in a meat grinder may seem like a lot of work for a cake, but this taste treat is certainly worth the extra effort. This cake is especially good when frosted with orange-flavored buttercream frosting, which is made by simply adding a teaspoon of orange extract to your buttercream recipe.

Preheat oven to 375°F.
Line an 11 × 17-inch sheet cake pan with parchment paper.

1½ cups salted peanuts with skins on	2 eggs
⅔ cup butter (at room temperature)	3½ cups sifted cake flour
	1½ teaspoons baking soda
2 cups sugar	2 teaspoons baking powder
	2 cups buttermilk

Grind the peanuts in a meat grinder or food processor. (If you use a food processor, be careful not to make creamy peanut butter!) In a large bowl, cream the softened butter and gradually add the sugar. Beat this mixture until it's light and fluffy. Add the eggs, one at a time, beating well after each addition. Sift dry ingredients into another bowl. Add dry ingredients alternately with buttermilk to butter-sugar-egg mixture. Be sure all ingredients are well blended. Add peanuts. Blend. (Be careful not to overbeat.) Pour batter into cake pan. Bake for 25 to 30 minutes, or until cake tester inserted into the center of the cake comes out clean. Cool at least one hour before decorating.

CUPCAKES

Personally, I would never bake cupcakes for someone's birthday. I think a cake is more fun. However, mothers often order cupcakes from Creative Cakes for a classroom or camp birthday party. Many schools encourage parents to let their elementary school children celebrate their birthdays at school; yet schools often won't permit children to bring cakes that have to be cut and served because they are too messy for the children to handle. You may be faced with the same problem.

There are many ways to spruce up cupcakes. If you're baking for a class, you could be making anywhere from fifteen to thirty cupcakes, so you'll probably want to keep them as simply decorated as possible. For example, you can make a round cupcake into the face of Raggedy Ann or Andy. Begin by frosting all the cupcakes with pale-pink frosting. Then with a No. 1 tip cone filled with black frosting, draw the eyes, eyebrows and mouth. With a cone filled with red frosting, make a triangle nose. Outline it in black. With orange frosting in a No. 3 tip cone, make raggedy hair. It's that easy.

Or you can just as easily put the insignia of Batman, Superman or any of the popular superheroes on each cupcake. You can write the child's name and age, or decorate cupcakes with any face you might imagine. You could make marzipan handles* and create tiny baskets. After you put the handles on the frosted cupcakes, you can top the cupcakes with tiny candies. Or you can make miniature flowers from frosting.

Another really simple thing to do is make the face of the cupcake look like a big daisy. You can also frost each one white and make baseballs by using a cone filled with red frosting to draw on the stitching lines. Give it some thought and you'll come up with all sorts of ideas. Even something as simple as the "smile" face against yellow frosting always brings delight to children.

By the way, never fill the cups in a muffin tin more than two-thirds full of batter. If you do, the cupcakes will rise over the top of your tin, making it difficult to get them out in one piece and also making them look as though you just threw them together. Neatness counts in cupcakes, too. I always use a tablespoon to measure how much I want in each cup. It's much easier and quicker than using a measuring cup for such a small amount. If you don't have

---

*If you make marzipan handles, be sure to think ahead. They should be prepared a week ahead of time. To make the handles, roll out marzipan the same way you made a snake from modeling clay when you were a child. The marizipan roll should be about ⅜ inch thick. Cut it into 7-inch lengths. Pinch each piece into a curve that will fit into a 2½-inch-wide cupcake. Allow your handles to harden at least a week in a dry place so they will hold their curved shape. Carefully turn them every couple of days.

enough batter for twelve cupcakes and your muffin tin has a dozen cups, fill the empty ones with a little water. This will prevent the empty cups from turning dark in the oven.

I also recommend using paper liners instead of greasing each cup. It's much easier. And the paper liners come in many colors, which gives the cupcakes a festive look. Also, I always use muffin tins with cups that are 2½ inches wide by 1¼ inches deep—the most standard size, and the one easiest to find paper liners for.

Lastly, any cake recipe can be used for cupcakes. I'm including a section of recipes for cupcakes because you don't need as large a recipe for cupcakes. Most of the time, the batter for a cupcake recipe will fit into an 8-inch square pan.

Chocolate Cupcakes

Preheat oven to 375°F.
Line 20–24 muffin-tin cups with paper liners.

3 1-ounce squares unsweetened chocolate	3 eggs
¾ cup boiling water	2¼ cups sifted cake flour
1½ teaspoons baking soda	1¼ teaspoons baking powder
⅓ cup margarine	¾ teaspoon salt
1½ cups sugar	½ cup sour cream

In the top part of a double boiler, heat chocolate squares until they are completely melted. Add boiling water and baking soda. Stir, and when blended, set aside to cool. In a large bowl, cream margarine and sugar with your electric mixer until fluffy. Add eggs, one at a time. Mix well. Into another bowl, sift dry ingredients. Add dry ingredients and sour cream alternately to the margarine-sugar mixture, blending after each addition. Add cooled chocolate mixture and stir until well blended. *Do not overbeat.* Pour into baking cups, filling each two-thirds full. Bake 25 to 30 minutes, or until cake tester inserted in the center of several cupcakes comes out clean. Let cool at least an hour before frosting.

Spice Cupcakes

Preheat oven to 375°F.
Line 12–15 muffin-tin cups with paper liners.

2 eggs	¾ teaspoon baking powder
1 cup light-brown sugar	1 teaspoon ground cinnamon
1¼ cups sifted all-purpose flour	½ teaspoon ground cloves
¼ teaspoon salt	1 cup sour cream

In a large bowl, beat eggs with an electric mixer until light. Gradually add sugar, blending well after each addition. In another bowl, sift all dry ingredients together. Then add dry ingredients and sour cream alternately to the egg-sugar mixture, mixing after each addition. Mix until smooth. Pour batter into baking cups, filling each cup two-thirds full. Bake 18 to 20 minutes, or until a cake tester inserted in the center of several of the cupcakes comes out clean. Cool at least an hour before frosting.

Yellow Cupcakes

Preheat oven to 375°F.
Line 15 muffin-tin cups with paper liners.

½ cup shortening (butter or margarine may be used)	2 teaspoons baking powder
1 cup sugar	¼ teaspoon salt
1 egg	⅔ cup milk
2 cups cake flour	1 teaspoon vanilla extract

In a large bowl, cream shortening thoroughly. Add sugar and mix until well blended. Add egg and continue mixing until light and fluffy. Sift dry ingredients into another bowl, and add them alternately to the mixture with milk and vanilla. Pour batter into 15 baking cups, filling each cup two-thirds full. Bake for 20 to 25 minutes, or until a cake tester inserted in the center of several of the cupcakes comes out clean. Let cool for at least an hour before frosting.

Aunt Frannie's Crazy Cupcakes

Here it is again. This is the same recipe that appeared earlier as a sheet cake. It's such a great recipe that I've cut it down here for cupcakes.

Preheat oven to 325°F.
Line 12–15 muffin-tin cups with paper liners.

1 cup sugar	½ teaspoon salt
1 egg	1 teaspoon baking powder
½ cup milk	½ teaspoon baking soda
½ cup cocoa	1 teaspoon vanilla extract
½ cup shortening (I use Crisco)	1½ cups all-purpose flour
	½ cup boiling water

In the order in which they are listed, place all ingredients except boiling water in a large bowl. Add boiling water, then stir until the mixture is smooth. Pour the batter into baking cups, filling each about two-thirds full. Bake for 20 to 25 minutes, or until a cake tester inserted in the center of several of the cupcakes comes out clean. Cool at least one hour before frosting.

FROSTINGS

There are many different kinds of cake frostings and fillings, but I always decorate my Creative Cakes with buttercream frosting. Seven-minute frosting, while it would make a nice background, sets too quickly for intricate cake decorating. Caramel or mocha frostings are fine if those are the major colors of your cake, but they obviously can't be colored. Buttercream needs no cooking and cannot be overbeaten. Besides, made-from-scratch buttercream frosting is a tasty treat!

I never keep frosting around for more than a week. With business as busy as it is, frosting never has a chance to stay around much longer than that. However, frosting will stay fresh for a couple of weeks if you keep it tightly covered in the refrigerator. It may just need a teaspoon or so of milk to thin it out and freshen it up a bit when you're ready to use it. Leftover frosting stored longer than a couple of weeks will begin to separate.

When you remove frosting from your refrigerator that's been stored for a while—even overnight—allow it to come to room temperature before you attempt to work with it. Don't try to soften your cold frosting by setting it in a warm oven. It won't soften evenly. Portions of it will become runny while the rest of it hasn't even begun to soften. Keep the frosting covered while it's softening, and stir it occasionally, remembering to recover it each time. If you don't cover it, the frosting will crystallize on top. Those crunchy little crystals can become a real nuisance when you're decorating. If your frosting does crystallize, try pushing it through a sieve with a rubber spatula and beating it again with your electric mixer. Unless the frosting is old and too crystallized, this procedure should make your frosting smooth and creamy once more.

The frosting recipes in this section are generous because you can't skimp when coloring frosting. Obviously, it's better to have too much than too little. In addition, the finishing touches on your cake will require extra frosting. Caulking edges and trim require more frosting. And you'll need at least half a cup of frosting for each color you use in decorating your cake. It takes about that much just to fill a cone once.

You're inevitably going to waste some frosting. Some is wasted because it sticks to the sides of the parchment paper cone that you dispose of when you're finished using it. You can unwrap every cone when you've finished with it, place it on a flat surface, and scrape away the unused frosting with a knife, but this practice is worthwhile only if you use a significant number of cones and the amount of frosting exceeds two or more cups. Otherwise, consider it scrap waste the way anyone with a hobby has waste.

If you do end up with a considerable amount of leftover frosting, you can mix it into chocolate frosting. When you mix all colors together, they turn a muddy gray/brown.* You must have at least 3 cups of frosting to make it worthwhile to mix chocolate this way. But when you do have enough leftover frosting, simply add ½ cup sifted cocoa, 1 tablespoon of butter or margarine, and a dash of salt until your leftover frosting is a rich chocolate brown. Add milk a teaspoon at a time. If you want to make a large batch of chocolate, keep adding more buttercream frosting and more of the cocoa mixture until you've got the amount you want. Beat the frosting until it's creamy and smooth with your electric mixer.

Buttercream Frosting

This recipe makes more than enough frosting for one 11 × 17-inch sheet cake, depending on how many colors are needed. You may want to cut it in half or double it as you become a better judge of your frosting needs. Remember, however, extra frosting is *far* better than too little.

½ **pound (2 sticks) butter or margarine *or* half butter and half margarine (softened to room temperature)**	½ **teaspoon salt**
	2 **teaspoons vanilla extract**
	2 **pounds (6–8 cups) confectioners' sugar**†
½ **cup milk**	

*If you ever have a large amount of *blue* frosting, don't add it to this mixture. Blue prevents a rich chocolatey color.

†You may have to add a little more or a little less depending on how settled your sugar is. If your sugar is old, you would be wise to sift it. Nothing is more frustrating than having a hard sugar lump clog the tip of a cone as soon as you begin to use it.

Place butter, milk, salt and vanilla in a large mixing bowl. Cover with about 3 cups of sugar. Begin mixing slowly so that sugar doesn't fly everywhere. Scrape the sides of the bowl from time to time. Gradually add the rest of the sugar. Continue beating until the mixture is light and fluffy. It will be an off-white color and creamy. Cover the frosting with a damp towel until you're ready to use it.

You may want to add a flavor extract to your frosting. Wagner's makes a great variety of pure extracts available in better supermarkets and gourmet shops. Add ½ teaspoon or to taste of peppermint, butter rum, orange or almond to flavor frosting for your cake when you want more flavor than buttercream. Such liqueurs as Grand Marnier, Amaretto, and Kahlúa will do the same trick. Can you imagine orange-flavored frosting that's colored blue?

Pure White Sugar Cream Frosting

I very seldom use pure white sugar cream frosting. Quite frankly, it's not very tasty. However, there are times when pure white frosting gives you the best contrast. For example, a cake shaped like a container of Johnson's baby powder can only be pure white. The same goes for the stars and stripes on Old Glory.

The best thing about this white frosting is that it keeps indefinitely in a tightly covered bowl in your refrigerator. It keeps much better than buttercream. It's also a good inexpensive frosting to use while you're practicing cake art on the bottom of a cake pan. You can save it and use it over and over again.

¾ cup vegetable shortening (I use Crisco)	½ teaspoon orange *or* lemon extract
¼ cup milk	1 pound (3–4 cups) confectioners' sugar
½ teaspoon salt	

Place shortening, milk, salt and extract in a large mixing bowl. Cover with about 2 cups of sugar. Begin mixing slowly so that sugar doesn't fly everywhere. Scrape the sides of the bowl from time to time. Gradually add the rest of the sugar. Continue beating until the mixture is light and fluffy. Cover the frosting with a damp towel until you're ready to use it. This recipe makes enough frosting for one 9 × 13-inch sheet cake.

Chocolate Buttercream Frosting

Make buttercream frosting according to the directions on page 49. Note the number of pounds of confectioners' sugar you use. For every pound of sugar used, allow:

6 to 8 tablespoons sifted cocoa

2 tablespoons softened butter or margarine

Dash of salt

Milk

In a large bowl, mix cocoa, butter and salt well. Then blend the cocoa mixture with prepared buttercream. Add milk a teaspoon at a time until your frosting is the right consistency for spreading smoothly.

If you need only a small amount of chocolate frosting, simply add cocoa and milk a teaspoon at a time to a small amount of plain buttercream frosting until the frosting is as chocolatey and creamy as you want.

Marzipan

1 cup almond paste* *or* 1 cup ground *blanched* almonds†

1 teaspoon almond extract

2 cups sifted confectioners' sugar

1 egg white

In a large bowl, combine almond paste, almond extract and sugar. In another bowl, beat the egg white until it is foamy and add it to the almond mixture. Knead the mixture with your hands until paste is smooth and pliable. (It should have the consistency of modeling clay.) Add more sugar if necessary to make paste easy to handle. It's easier to mix this up one recipe at a time instead of doubling or tripling it because it's hard to mix it thoroughly in large amounts. Knead it all together once you have all the batches mixed.

Color the marzipan as you would frosting, adding a toothpick tip full of color at a time until you get the shade you desire.

FAVORITE DESSERTS

When I'm having a dinner party, I like to surprise my guests with a dessert other than cake. In fact, I think it's almost corny for me to serve cake unless, of course, it's a birthday dinner.

*Almond paste can usually be found in the gourmet section of the supermarket.
†Put the almonds through a meat grinder or food processor three or four times.

It seems I'm always short of time. And since I like to make everything fresh and from scratch, I can't often spend a lot of time preparing fancy desserts. Therefore, I have several yummy time-saving dessert recipes. Any of them can be whipped up in less than half an hour (not counting cooking time) except for the apple crumb pie. (I do make exceptions during apple season!)

I hope you'll enjoy these few recipes when a creative cake doesn't fit into your schedule or your dinner plans.

Zucchini Bread

Many years ago my Aunt Marjorie's zucchini crop was so plentiful that she searched for a way other than freezing to use up her zucchini. She came up with zucchini bread. It has the spicy flavor and moistness of carrot cake and is expecially delicious right from the oven, cooled and spread with cream cheese or sliced and toasted with butter. It's also fun to ask people to guess what the main ingredient is.

Preheat oven to 325°F.
Grease and flour 2 bread-loaf pans.

1⅔ to 2 cups sugar	1 cup oil
1 tablespoon cinnamon	2 cups grated unpeeled zuc-
3 cups all-purpose flour	chini
1 teaspoon baking soda	1 tablespoon vanilla extract
½ teaspoon baking powder	½ cup chopped pecans
1 teaspoon salt	½ cup raisins (optional)
3 eggs	

Into a large bowl, sift dry ingredients. Set aside. In another bowl, mix the eggs, oil, zucchini and vanilla. Add this mixture to the dry ingredients and blend well. Stir in pecans and raisins. Pour the batter into pans. Bake about an hour (checking after 45 minutes), or until a cake tester inserted in the center of the loaves comes out clean.

Apple Surprise

When I was a kid spending my summer vacations on my grandparents' farm just outside Battle Ground, Indiana, my grandmother taught me this apple surprise. I especially enjoyed it when we topped it with the frozen custard from a nearby stand. We served it often as a simple and quick dessert for the hired hands when they came in for lunch during the August hay baling time. It's still one of my favorite desserts, and as a bonus, it's comparatively low in calories.

Preheat oven to 350°F.
Grease and flour 9-inch *pie* pan.

⅔ cup sugar
½ cup all-purpose flour
1 teaspoon baking powder
    Dash of salt
1 well-beaten egg

½ cup chopped walnuts or pecans
1 cup cored, peeled and chopped apples

Sift dry ingredients, and add egg. Stir in nuts and apples. Pour into pie pan. Bake about 30 minutes, or until a cake tester inserted into the center comes out clean. Serves five or six people and is terrific with ice cream or whipped cream.

Banana Cream Pie

You'll have to try this banana pie to believe it. It's like no other banana cream pie. It's delicately rich. A large portion is not necessary, though after the first bite, desire may overwhelm necessity.

While this pie doesn't take long to prepare, its rich flavor results from chilling in the refrigerator *at least twelve* hours. There's no way to hurry up the flavor, so plan ahead. And by the way, don't let the shortening scare you away! No one will *ever* guess it's there.

Prepare and bake a 9-inch pie shell.

1½ cups confectioners' sugar
½ cup shortening (I use Crisco)
2 eggs

1 teaspoon vanilla extract
2 diced bananas
1 1-ounce bar of milk chocolate

In a large bowl, beat sugar and shortening until light and fluffy with an electric beater. (A blender will *not* work.) Add one egg. Beat until fluffy. Add the other egg. Beat again. Add vanilla. Fold in bananas. Pour the mixture into *prebaked* pie shell. Shave the bar of milk chocolate over the top of the pie by using the slicer on your vegetable grater or peeler. Chill 10 to 12 hours. Makes 6 to 8 servings.

Apple Crumb Pie

Apple crumb pie is a favorite of mine every apple season. It's delicious all by itself or with a slice of cheddar cheese. But it's best with a big scoop of vanilla ice cream!

Preheat oven to 400°F.
Prepare a 9-inch pie shell.

1 cup sugar	¾ cup all-purpose flour
1 teaspoon cinnamon	½ cup butter
6–8 tart apples (about 3 cups), pared, cored and sliced	½ cup chopped pecans

In a small bowl, mix ½ cup sugar with cinnamon. Sprinkle half the sugar mixture on bottom of pie shell. In a large bowl, mix apples and remaining cinnamon mixture. Fill the pie crust with apples. In another bowl mix the remaining ½ cup sugar, flour, and butter. Sprinkle over top of pie. Bake at 400° for 10 minutes, then reduce temperature to 350°. After the pie has been in the oven for 30 minutes, sprinkle pecans over the pie. (It's important not to top the pie with pecans for the entire baking time. If you do, they will burn.) Continue baking until pecans are brown and apples are done.

Pecan Pie

In my opinion, a pecan pie is one of the easiest pies around. It's delicious any time, but because it's so heavy and rich, it's especially good around the holidays or in cooler weather.

Preheat oven to 350°F.
Prepare 9-inch pie shell.

⅔ cup sugar	1 cup dark corn syrup (I use Karo)
3 eggs, well-beaten	1 cup pecan halves
⅓ cup butter	1 teaspoon vanilla extract
Dash of salt	

In a large bowl, add sugar to eggs and mix thoroughly. Melt butter in a small saucepan and add it to the egg mixture. Mix well. Blend the rest of the ingredients into the sugar-egg mixture. Mix, being sure to coat all the pecans. Pour batter into pastry shell. (You may want to turn all the pecan halves outside up.) Bake for about 50 minutes, or until knife comes out clean when inserted in the center of the pie. Cool. Serve with fresh whipped cream.

4

Sixteen Creative Cakes

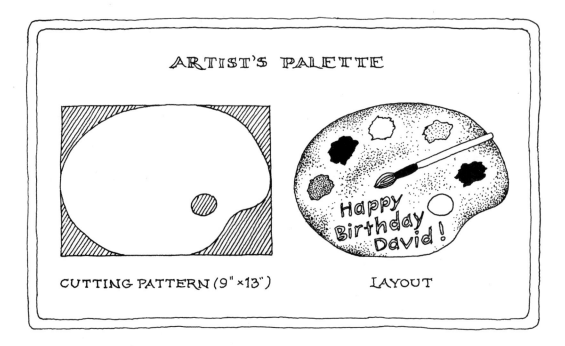

ARTIST'S PALETTE

CUTTING PATTERN (9" ×13")   LAYOUT

The sixteen Creative Cakes in this chapter are meant to serve as jumping-off points for your own unique creative cakes. You might do well to read through the instructions for a number of these suggested cakes before you begin any cake of your own because some of them feature helpful tricks and techniques. I recommend that for your very first cake you stick to something simple and follow one of my suggested cakes fairly closely. Once you have the feel of things, and have mastered the basic techniques, you'll be able to create your own unique cake for any occasion!

ARTIST'S PALETTE CAKE

An artist's palette cake is an easy cake full of color. The addition of a three-dimensional paintbrush made from marzipan and personalized with the artist's name gives your work a special touch.

1. Bake a 9 × 13-inch sheet cake (6 cups batter). Set the cake aside to cool at least an hour.
2. Meanwhile, cover a 10 × 14-inch board.
3. Prepare half a recipe of buttercream frosting (see p. 49).
4. Make a paper pattern according to the illustration.
5. Place pattern on the cake, which is still in the pan, and cut cake along the edge of the pattern. Place your cake on the serving board.
6. With a No. 3 or 4 tip cone filled with uncolored buttercream frosting, draw an oval where the thumb should go. Fill it in with more buttercream frosting.
7. Now set aside about a cup of frosting for the colors.
8. Add a little cocoa powder to the remaining buttercream frosting to make a pale brown so your artist's palette looks like it's made of wood. Spread the cake with the light brown. You may want to streak it to give it a wood-grain appearance.
9. Now mix eight or so bright colors, or use leftover frosting you may have saved from previous cakes. Dab the frosting at random around the cake's surface. Easy as that.
10. Be sure to caulk around the bottom of the cake next to the serving board with a No. 5 tip cone.

11. Now take some marzipan to make a paintbrush. Color it, if you want. Roll it out until it's about 8 inches long and taper it to look like the handle of a paintbrush. Place it on the cake. With a No. 1 tip cone filled with black frosting, draw the bristles. And personalize the brush by writing the artist's name on it with the same cone.

WATERMELON CAKE

What summer picnic would be complete without watermelon? At this year's first outing, why not surprise your family and friends with a slice-of-watermelon cake. Or perhaps replace your annual American flag cake at the neighborhood Fourth of July picnic with another American tradition. And with a watermelon cake, you won't have to spit out the seeds!

1. Bake a 9 × 13-inch oblong sheet cake (5 cups of batter). Place it on a rack to cool for at least an hour.
2. Meanwhile, prepare one recipe of buttercream frosting (see p. 49).
3. Cover a 15 × 9-inch piece of cardboard.
4. After the cake has cooled sufficiently, make a paper pattern according to the illustration and cut the cake.
5. Place piece 1 on your covered serving board. Frost it with uncolored buttercream.
6. Now take piece 2 and place it on top of the frosted curve of piece 1.
7. Butt pieces 3 and 4 against piece 2.
8. Using a long sharp bread knife, shave the cake so it is at a slant. Make sure the slant is smooth. Use the extra pieces of cake to fill in, but always spread frosting between layers of cake to hold the layers together and to prevent a problem with crumbs in your frosting.
9. Before coloring your frosting, drop a No. 8 metal tip into a cone and fill it with uncolored frosting.
10. Now color half of the remaining frosting bright green and half of it hot pinkish red. If you don't have marzipan, you'll also need some black frosting for the seeds, but you can use either of your leftover colors for that. No need to do it now.
11. Cover the top slant with pink frosting. Spread the frosting gently. Because there are so many raw edges, you may have trouble with crumbs if you're not careful.
12. Next, spread the edges with green to look like the rind. Spread the

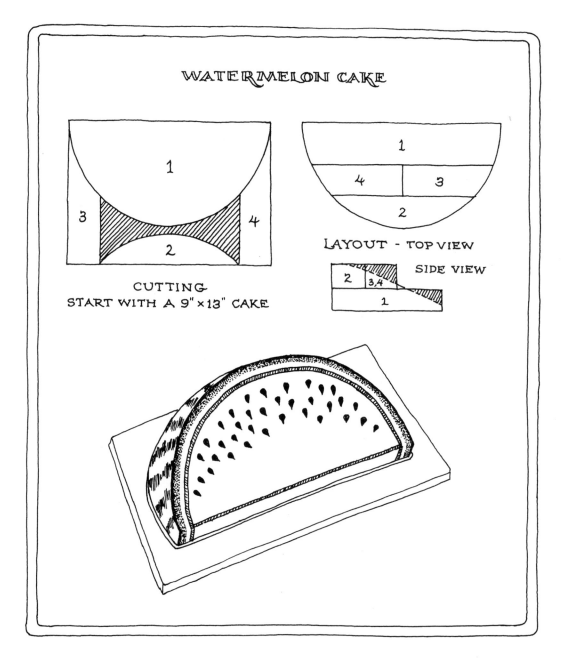

WATERMELON CAKE

1

3

2

4

CUTTING
START WITH A 9" × 13" CAKE

1

4

3

2

LAYOUT - TOP VIEW

SIDE VIEW

2

3,4

1

green just over the top edge of the cake until it meets the pink. Completely frost the sides of the cake.

13. Caulk bottom edges with pink and green to match.

14. Now take the white cone you made earlier and draw a wide line where the green and the pink meet. With a slightly moistened knife or spatula, smooth the white so that it blends on the edges with the green and the pink. If you can visualize the way a slice of watermelon looks (the rind gets paler toward the center), you'll have an advantage. Also, streak the outside rind of the cake with the white cone. Carefully smooth the frosting streaks with a moistened knife to create uneven streaks. Again, if you can imagine how a watermelon rind looks, your cake will appear more realistic.

15. Last of all, color marzipan with black food coloring. Shape it into many tiny seeds. Stick them randomly on the pink part of the watermelon. If you don't have marzipan, never fear: simply color some leftover frosting with black food coloring and draw on the seeds with a No. 3 tip cone. And now you have a slice-of-watermelon cake!

TRAIN CAKE

This cake will serve fifteen to twenty children. You will need licorice sticks, jelly beans or gumdrops, licorice discs for the coal car, and any other brightly colored candy or marzipan to serve as cargo.*

1. Bake your favorite recipe in a 13 × 9 × 2-inch oblong pan. (That's the same recipe that may tell you to bake your cake in two 8- or 9-inch round pans.)

2. Cut and cover a 20 × 24-inch serving board.

3. Prepare one recipe of buttercream frosting (see p. 49).

4. Make paper patterns according to the illustrations, and after the cake has cooled at least an hour, cut it out according to the numbered layout. There will be enough cake here for five cars: a locomotive, a coal car, two flatcars, a cattle or freight car, and a caboose. Arrange pattern pieces for the cars on the board in an interesting layout.

5. Prepare red frosting for the caboose, black frosting for the engine, and frosting in other colors of your choice for the other cars. You may want to make them all the same color. You'll need one large black gumdrop for the engine. And Life Savers for the wheels.

*If you have leftover candy, seal it in its package and tightly seal it a second time in a plastic bag. It should stay fresh until the next time you need it.

TRAIN CAKE

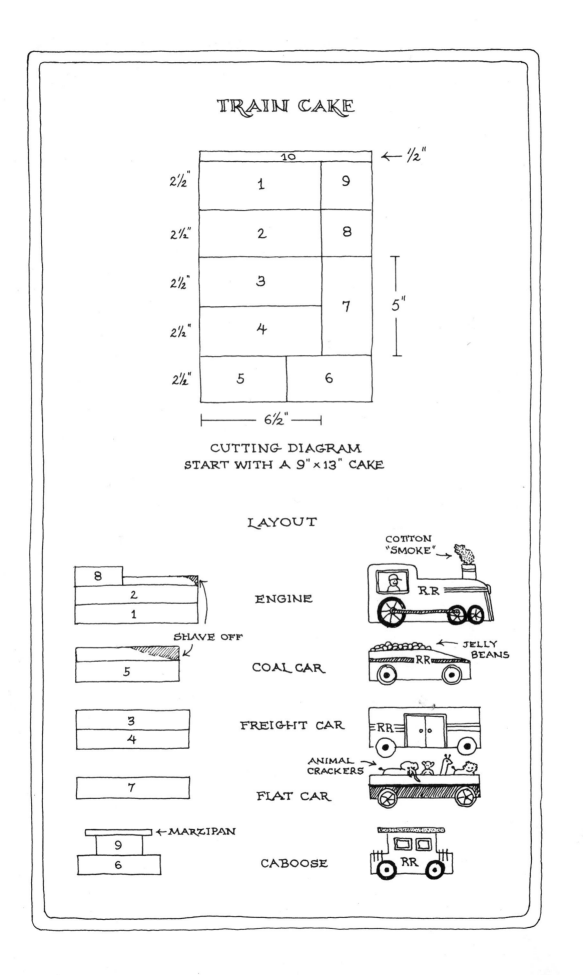

CUTTING DIAGRAM
START WITH A 9" × 13" CAKE

LAYOUT

ENGINE

COTTON "SMOKE"

RR

SHAVE OFF

COAL CAR

JELLY BEANS

RR

FREIGHT CAR

RR

ANIMAL CRACKERS

FLAT CAR

MARZIPAN

CABOOSE

RR

6. Begin by placing the bottom engine piece (piece 1) of cake in its proper place. Spread frosting between pieces 1 and 2, with piece 8 at one end. You will notice when you cut out your pieces that there's a ½-inch wide end (piece 10). Cut off a 3½-inch strip of it and place cake edge side up on the front of the engine. When it's frosted, it will give the front of the engine a slightly rounded appearance. Now frost the engine with black frosting. Use white frosting to draw the windows; make them square by outlining them with black frosting. When these are finished, take a No. 5 tip cone filled with black frosting and finish the bottom edge as though you were caulking to prevent leakage. Take your large black gumdrop and place it where the smokestack should be.

7. When you make the coal car (piece 5), use the last chunk of piece 10, the leftover edge, to give the car a slight slant. Frost it the desired color and fill the top with licorice candy. Finish it by caulking just as you did the engine.

8. Continue to decorate the cars one by one, following the illustration. Fill the flatcar with different candies.

9. Color 3-inch ball of marzipan with the same color you used to frost the caboose. With a rolling pin, roll out a 7 × 3¼-inch rectangle of marzipan. Square the corners by cutting with a knife. After you've frosted the caboose, place the marzipan on top to create the overhang of the roof.

10. Now you are ready to make the train track. You'll need seven licorice sticks 4½ inches long. Cut the rest of the licorice into 1½-inch-long pieces. Arrange the licorice sticks around the train, sticking the 1½-inch pieces ½ inch into the cake. Secure the larger pieces on the board by putting a dab of frosting underneath them. Add the Life Saver wheels.

11. Finally, with a No. 2 tip cone, use a contrasting color to write the child's name (for example, "Donnie's R.R." or "Rachel's Birthday Express") on the engine. Write his or her age on the cars. Draw doors and perhaps a ladder on the freight car.

SNEAKERS CAKE

1. Bake an 11 × 17-inch oblong cake.
2. Make a 14 × 20-inch covered serving board.
3. Prepare one recipe of buttercream frosting (see p. 49).
4. While your cake is cooling, make your paper pattern by tracing around a pair of your sneakers. Trace the rear half of each shoe twice to make two additional pieces (see illustration).
5. Place the patterns on your cake. Cut around them. Be sure to have

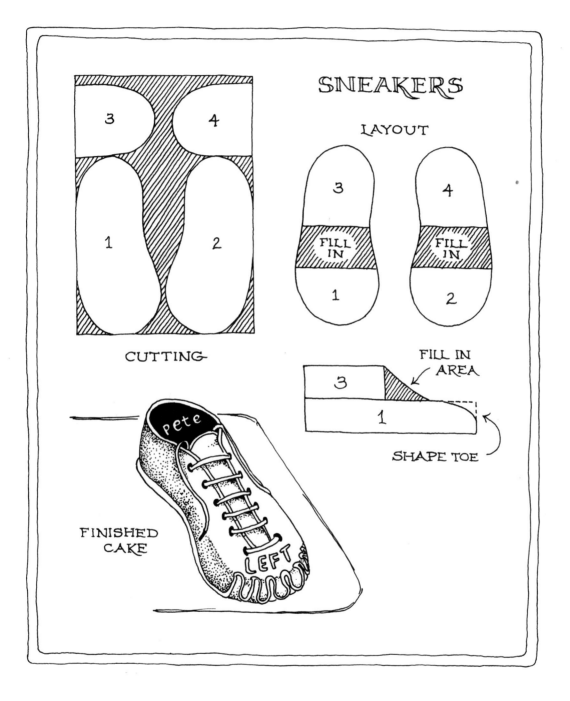

SNEAKERS

LAYOUT

3   4

1   2

FILL IN   FILL IN

CUTTING

FILL IN AREA

3

1

SHAPE TOE

FINISHED CAKE

pete

LEFT

a right and a left foot. Or if the person is notably clumsy, you might want two left feet!

6. Place the two bottom layers (pieces 1 and 2) on your covered serving board.

7. Frost the back half of these layers.

8. Place the second layer (pieces 3 and 4) on top, and with the scraps, fill in to give the sneaker an angled appearance. You may also need to shave off some of the cake to make it smooth and slanted.

9. Mix about a cup of chocolate frosting (see p. 51) and frost the back part of the shoe where the foot would enter with chocolate frosting.

10. Now frost the rest of the sneaker with uncolored buttercream.

11. With a No. 10 tip cone, outline around the tongue and the edges of the shoe and indicate the seams and the lines of the sneaker. Make ripply curves on the front of the sneaker to indicate reinforcement. I usually use uncolored buttercream for these steps, but you could also use a contrasting color.

12. Using a contrasting color in a medium-sized cone, make dots for the shoelace holes.

13. Again, with the No. 10 cone, make the laces. You may want to use white or another contrasting color.

14. I always write my message on the chocolate section where the foot would enter the shoe. People have wanted such messages as "I hope you get a kick out of this," "Put your best foot forward," and "Only the world's best _____ could fill these shoes."

Sometimes I add stripes on the sides and across the toe. Once I put "right" and "left" on the appropriate feet. Oftentimes customers bring in the shoes they want me to copy! You may have a special pair of sneakers you want to duplicate, too.

BASEBALL MITT CAKE

This cake is a favorite of baseball fans of any age, though I find it most popular for children's summer parties. Cupcakes decorated to look like baseballs can be made to accompany the mitt cake and will insure a "home run" with the kids.

1. Bake an 8-inch square cake and use the rest of the batter for cupcakes.

2. While your cake is cooling, make a paper pattern by drawing around your hand. Cut out the pattern.

BASEBALL MITT *and* BALL

CUTTING

PLACE BALL (2) ON
MITT AND FROST

3. Make a 10 × 14-inch covered cardboard serving board.

4. Prepare half a recipe of buttercream frosting (see p. 49).

5. Cut your cake according to the pattern.

6. Color 4 cups of your frosting chocolate or caramel color (a mixture of yellow, red and brown food coloring) or any other color that you want the mitt to be.

7. Frost the mitt.

8. Finish the bottom edge of the mitt with a No. 7 tip cone as though you were caulking.

9. Use licorice laces to make the laces on the mitt. Or else draw them on with black frosting in a No. 6 tip cone.

10. Take three cupcakes out of their papers, and frost them with white frosting. You now have three baseballs to place around the mitt.

11. With a decorating cone filled with black frosting, using a No. 1 or 2 tip, make stitches on the mitt and on the baseball.

12. Either use piece 2 cut from the square of cake or unwrap a fourth cupcake and place it in the palm of the mitt. Frost it with white frosting, and decorate it to look like a baseball, too.

13. An autographed mitt shows authenticity and status, so you may want to be clever and sign the child's name in frosting on the bottom of the palm of the mitt. Writing the word "Official" beneath the name will add a professional touch and will make the baseball mitt a big hit with your Little Leaguer.

Finally, what about all the rest of the cupcakes? If there will be a lot of children at your party, you may want to decorate the top of each cupcake with baseball stitching and again sign the child's name. If not, frost and freeze the rest of your baking as a special treat for another day.

SCULPTURED BUNNY CAKE

The bunny cake is suitable for several occasions. Consider it for a baby shower, Easter, someone named Bunny or someone who does laboratory research.

1. You should make your marzipan ears a few days before you need your cake, so the marzipan will harden and hold its shape. Color the marzipan pale pink. Shape into two ears about four inches long, about 1½ inches wide at the widest point. Allow them to harden in a dry place. If you don't have marzipan, you can make the ears from heavy paper, although I try to stay away from nonedible products on my cakes.

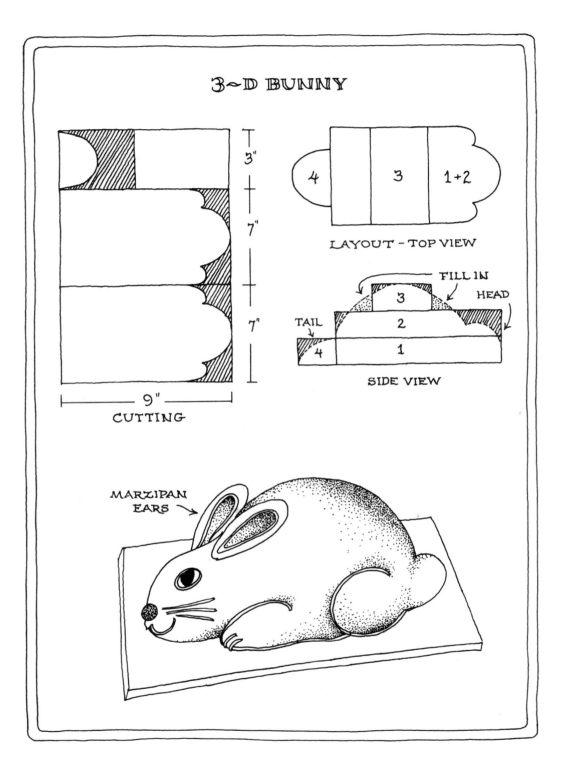

3~D BUNNY

3"

7"

7"

9"

CUTTING

LAYOUT - TOP VIEW

4

3

1 + 2

FILL IN

HEAD

TAIL

3

2

1

4

SIDE VIEW

MARZIPAN
EARS

2. Bake a 13 × 9-inch cake.

3. Prepare one recipe of pure white sugar cream frosting (see p. 50).

4. Cover a 10 × 12-inch serving board.

5. Make a paper pattern according to the diagram.

6. Cut the cake according to the pattern.

7. Place the first two layers (pieces 1 and 2) on the board, frosting between the layers.

8. Frost the top.

9. Place the third layer (piece 3) two inches from the back of the bunny.

10. Place the tail piece (piece 4) in back. Use a sharp bread knife to shave and carve as you round the top and give your cake a bunny shape. Use your cake scraps to fill in areas wherever needed, adhering cake to cake with frosting.

11. Before the frosting has a chance to set, cover the rabbit with *flake* coconut.

12. Use pink jelly beans or a decorating cone filled with pink frosting for the eyes and nose.

13. Frost the back of the marzipan ears with white frosting. This is a messy job. I usually lay the ears face down on my work surface and frost.

14. Secure the ears by carefully sticking them into the bunny's head.

15. To make grass to arrange around the bunny, put about two cups of *shredded* coconut in a small bowl. Thoroughly dissolve some green paste food coloring in several teaspoons of water. The amount of food coloring you use will determine the color of your coconut. (By the way, if you happen to have some liquid food coloring from your old cake decorating days, here's a chance to use it up.) Pour the dissolved food coloring over your coconut. Mix with your hands until the coconut is thoroughly colored. You may have to add a bit more food coloring to make the color brighter, but be careful not to add too much moisture to the already moist coconut.

16. Finally, spread some frosting around the bunny. Pat the colored coconut on top of the frosting and slightly up the sides of the bunny to make him look as though he's sitting in the grass. If the cake is for Easter, you might want to hide jelly beans or candy eggs in the grass, too.

FLAT BUNNY CAKE

If you don't feel daring enough to attempt a three-dimensional shape, you could try this bunny face that I watched sixteen-year-old Krissy create in less than an hour after her cakes had been baked and cooled.

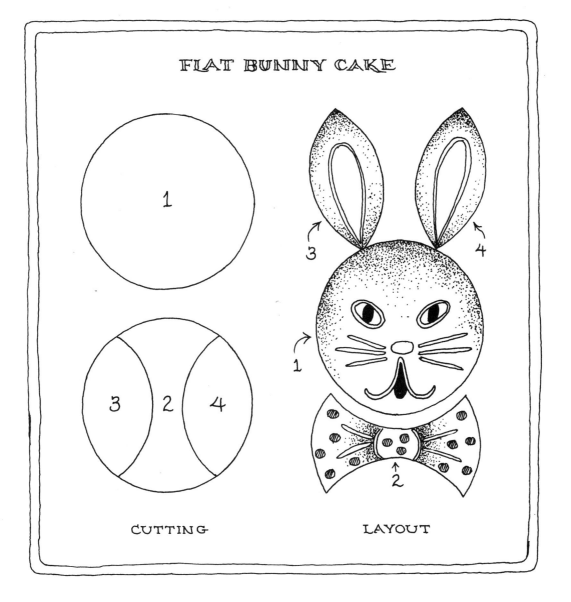

FLAT BUNNY CAKE

CUTTING   LAYOUT

1. Bake two 9-inch round cakes.
2. Make a bunny pattern according to the diagram.
3. Cover a 22 × 11-inch piece of cardboard.
4. Make one recipe of pure white sugar cream frosting (see p. 50).
5. Lay out the bunny on your board as illustrated.
6. Frost the bunny with pure white frosting.
7. Color some frosting pink and frost the insides of the ears and the bow tie. (Or you can mix another color for the bow tie.)
8. Using a No. 3 tip cone filled with black frosting, draw whiskers. Or if you have licorice laces, you can make whiskers from them.
9. Make the eyes from gumdrops or jelly beans.
10. You can also dot the bow tie with jelly beans. Or if you'd like, make several colors and fill No. 2 or 3 tip cones to make a plaid bow tie.
11. Draw the mouth with the cone filled with pink frosting.

JOHNSON'S BABY POWDER CAKE

This cake is pretty and easy to make. It's a wonderful cake for a new mother or for a baby shower for a mother-to-be.

1. Bake a 9 × 13-inch cake.
2. Make a covered 7 × 15-inch serving board.
3. Prepare a batch of pure white sugar cream frosting (see p. 50).
4. Cut the cake in half lengthwise.
5. Frost piece 1 and lay piece 2 on top.
6. To form the cap of the container, about 1 inch from the top, cut down about ½ an inch (see the diagram). Now cut about ½ inch from each side.
7. Frost the cake.
8. Mix about 1½ cups of blue frosting.
9. Fill Nos. 2 and 3 tip cones, each with about half the blue frosting.
10. Prepare 1 cup of pink frosting.
11. Fill a No. 2 tip cone with the pink frosting.
12. Using the actual product or an advertisement for Johnson's baby powder as your model, copy the layout and design on the container. If you

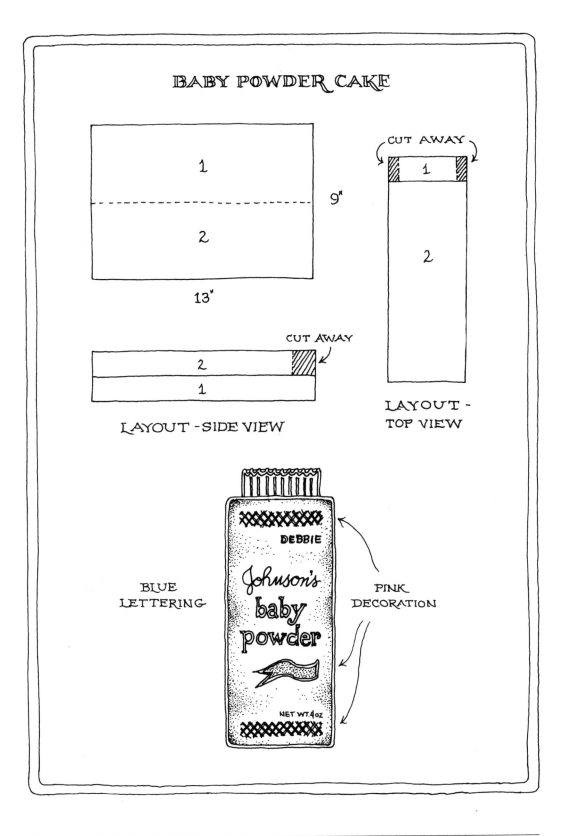

BABY POWDER CAKE

LAYOUT - SIDE VIEW

LAYOUT - TOP VIEW

BLUE LETTERING

PINK DECORATION

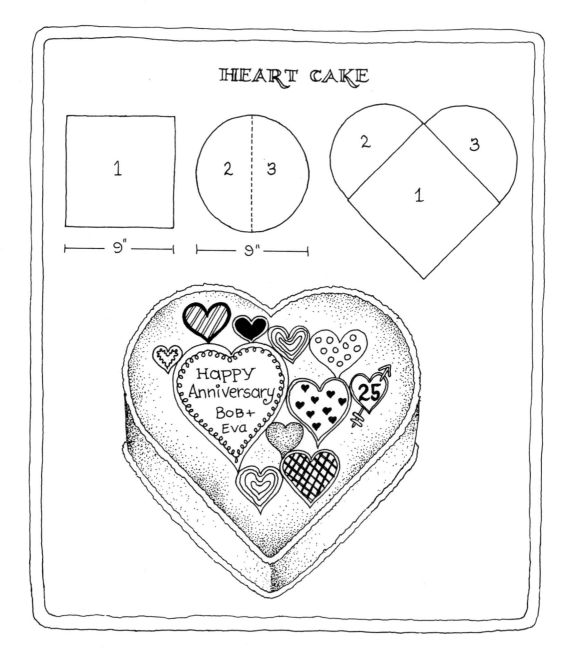

HEART CAKE

doubt your ability to letter in a straight line, you may want to use a string as your guide (see p. 22). Where it says "purest protection" on the pink flag, I usually write a message such as "Happy Parenthood."

13. Caulk the edges with a No. 7 tip cone, and with the same cone, make vertical ridges on the lid. And there you have a cake almost as precious as the baby it's honoring.

HEART-SHAPE CAKE

I seldom have use for a heart-shaped cake, so I don't have any heart-shaped pans. You may not have one either. And why should you invest in one? They're expensive, and once you go "creative," you probably won't have much need for one. Here's an easy way to cut a heart from regular baking pans: Bake one 9-inch round cake and one 9-inch square cake. Cut the round cake in half. Lay the cake out as the illustration shows by placing the halves against two adjacent sides of the square cake. Now you have a heart. Frost it.

TENNIS RACQUET CAKE

Every tennis player will love a tennis racquet cake. The thing that makes it the most fun is that it's the size of the actual tennis racquet. It looks as though you could pick it up and play with it. Moreover, the added touch of a ball alongside it makes it a sure hit.

1. Bake an 11 × 17-inch sheet cake (8 cups of batter). Let it cool at least an hour.

2. Make a paper pattern by drawing around your tennis racquet (or squash racquet or racquet-ball racquet). When you get to the shaft and the grip area, make your pattern about 1½ inches wide.

3. Make an 11 × 28-inch serving board.

4. Prepare one recipe of buttercream frosting (see p. 49).

5. Cut out the racquet from your cake by following the illustration. You will have to piece the handle together, so save the leftover pieces.

6. Lay out your tennis racquet cake on the serving board.

7. Color half of your frosting chocolate or any other color you want to use on the head of the racquet. The strings and the head of the racquet must be frosted in contrasting colors.

TENNIS RACQUET CAKE

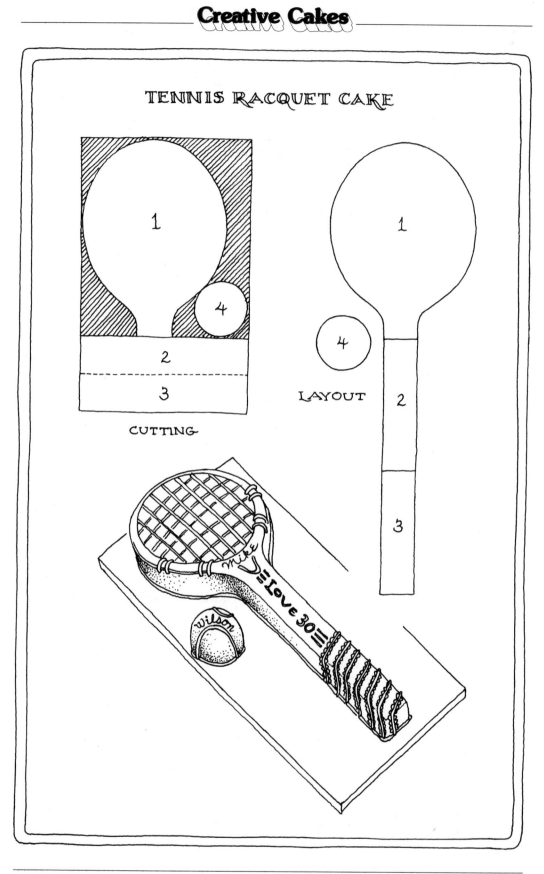

CUTTING

LAYOUT

8. After you've frosted the head, fill a No. 3 tip cone with a contrasting color and draw the string lines across the head, making sure the string lines are straight. Then draw the vertical strings.

9. Next, mix enough frosting to frost the sides of the head and the handle. (Sometimes I simply add white frosting to my leftover chocolate to make a paler chocolate. That way I use up most of my frosting.)

10. Fill a No. 9 tip cone. Now draw around the head, covering up the string ends.

11. Frost the sides. Smooth the frosting.

12. With another contrasting color and a No. 6 tip cone, make diagonal lines on the grip to simulate a taped look.

13. Draw stripes in appropriate places on the head of the racquet to indicate the tape.

14. Now cut a round piece the size of a cupcake from your leftovers. This will be your tennis ball.

15. With either white or yellow-green—the color of the fluorescent tennis balls—frosting cover the small cake.

16. Caulk around the bottom edges of both the racquet and the ball to seal in freshness.

17. Finally, with a No. 1 or 2 tip cone and contrasting colors, decorate the racquet with the logo of the brand the player uses. Or else write messages like "Pro" or "Champ" or "We love your racquet." Be clever. There are many tennis terms that can be used in writing your message. So get set! And have a ball!

SPRING BONNET CAKE

This cake makes a wonderful tasty welcome to spring. I like to decorate the hatband with colorful marzipan flowers, but you might prefer a different style hat decorated with fruit, feathers or whatever is appropriate to your occasion.

1. Make a 16-inch round (8 cups of batter) cake. Also make two 8-inch round cakes. (If you don't have 8-inch pans, cut 9-inch cakes down.)

2. Prepare a recipe of buttercream frosting (see p. 49).

3. Make an 18-inch square serving board.

4. Assemble the cake according to the diagram, spreading frosting between the layers.

5. Frost the entire surface of the cake with any color buttercream frosting. The natural color of the buttercream frosting, an off-white, makes a lovely hat.

SPRING BONNET

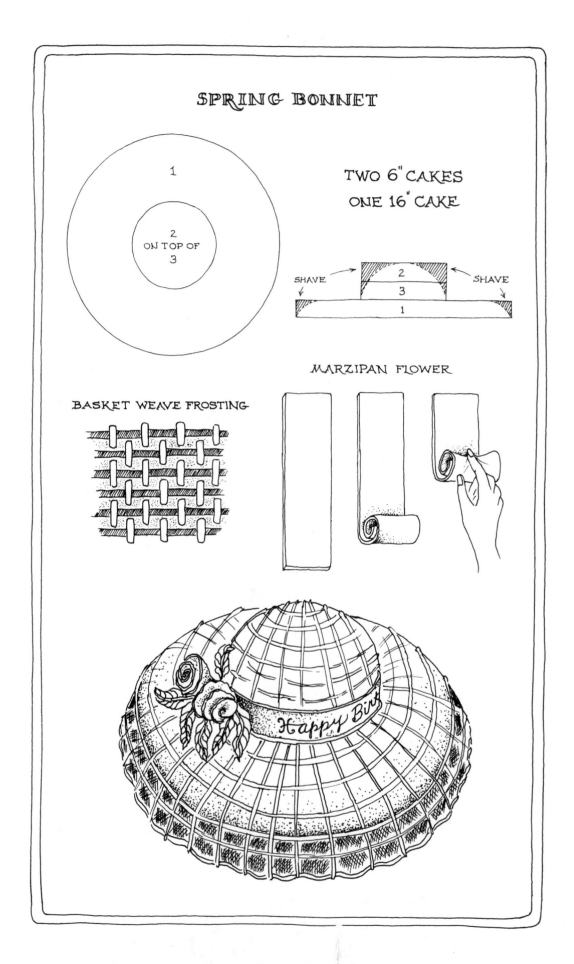

1

2
ON TOP OF
3

TWO 6" CAKES
ONE 16" CAKE

SHAVE   2   SHAVE
3
1

MARZIPAN FLOWER

BASKET WEAVE FROSTING

Happy Bir

6. With a medium-sized tip (a No. 5 is fine) cone, draw a line around the crown of the hat where the band should be.

7. With a No. 7 tip cone, make horizontal lines about ½ inch apart all around the brim from the crown to the edge. Keep your lines as equidistant from each other as possible.

8. Now do a basket stitch from the crown to the edge of the brim (see the illustration). Continue this technique until the entire brim is decorated.* Caulk the edge.

9. Now decorate the top of the crown with the same stitch.

10. Carefully spread frosting on the area where the band should be with the same or a contrasting color.

11. Now color some marzipan with any color that would make a pretty flower. A ball about 2 inches in diameter will be enough.

12. Roll out the marzipan with a rolling pin till it's about 8 inches long and 2 inches wide or until the marzipan is about ¼ inch thick.

13. Loosen underneath with a thin spatula so it won't stick to your work area. Now begin to roll it up. Once the roll is begun, gently pinch the center of the roll with your finger. Continue to roll while applying pressure to the middle. That way, the edges of the roll will begin to open into two roses.

14. When you come to the end, cut the roll of marzipan in half to form two flowers.

15. Place the flowers on one side of the hat next to the crown.

16. Now put a No. 68 leaf tip in a cone and fill it with green frosting. Practice making a few leaves before you put any on your cake. When you've got it right, make leaves around the flowers. If you don't have a leaf tip, you can simply use a medium-sized tip cone to outline and color your leaves.

17. Finally, with a No. 1 tip cone, delicately write the message on the hatband.

CLOWN CAKE

The clown cake is very simple to make. It's a good cake to make with children: because so many of the decorations are candy, you avoid the sticky mess of

---

*If you ever want to make a simple basket cake, stack two or three square or round layers on top of each other. Follow the directions for the basket stitch around the sides. Make a handle from hardened marzipan. Fill the basket with marzipan fruits or draw spring flowers with frosting.

CUTTING

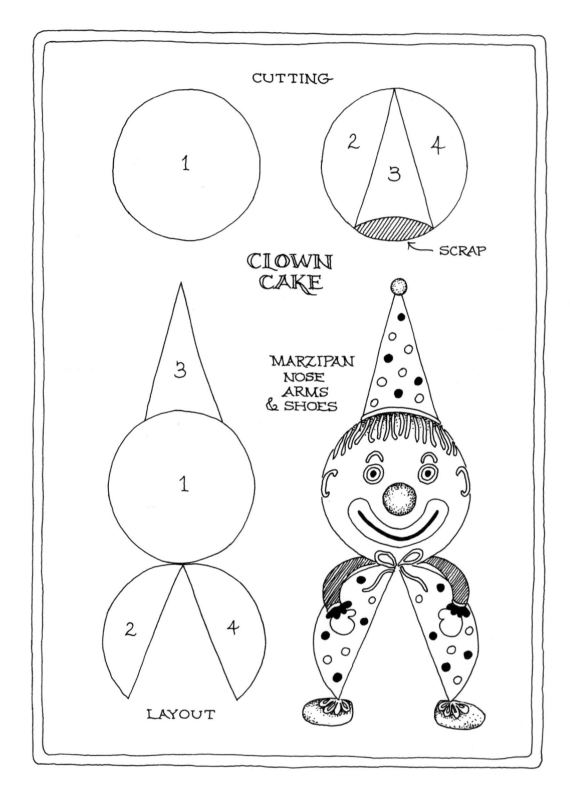

SCRAP

CLOWN
CAKE

MARZIPAN
NOSE
ARMS
& SHOES

LAYOUT

frosting. It also demands limited artistic skills. And as one *Romper Room* appearance taught me, children love to roll out the marzipan for the raggedy hair and to add the colored candies to the hat and the body. The clown is an appropriate cake for a circus party or one in which you've invited a clown to help you entertain your little ones.

1. Mix enough batter of your favorite recipe to fill two round pans. You can use any size pans you wish (these instructions are for 9-inch pans). Bake and set aside to cool.

2. Prepare one recipe of buttercream frosting (see p. 49).

3. You'll need 7 ounces of marzipan. Color it red with food coloring. You'll also need colored sugar-coated chocolate candies *or* gumdrops and white Life Savers.

4. Cover a 28 × 11-inch serving board.

5. When your cake has cooled, cut according to the illustration. Assemble on the serving board, following the illustration. There will be one small scrap piece.

6. Fill a No. 7 tip cone with white frosting.

7. Color one-third of the frosting a flesh color using a combination of pink and yellow coloring.

8. Color the remaining frosting any color. I chose yellow.

9. Make two No. 5 tip cones. Fill one with flesh-colored frosting and the other with yellow.

10. Spread flesh frosting over the face area of the cake.

11. Spread yellow frosting over the body and hat areas.

12. Clean up the board around the cake. Caulk the edges with matching colored frosting.

13. Color some leftover frosting black. Fill a No. 2 tip cone. Outline the cake.

14. Dot the hat and body with colored candies.

15. Place a 1½-inch marzipan ball nose in the center of the face.

16. Make rosy cheeks with dabs of red frosting.

17. Draw a large mouth with white frosting.

18. Add Life Saver eyes. Fill hole with black frosting.

19. Roll out marzipan for arms. Form "snakes" of marzipan into C shapes for arms. Put in place on cake, following illustration.

20. Form two egg-shaped feet from marzipan. Put in place.

21. Draw on shoelaces with a black frosting cone.

22. Roll out the rest of the marzipan into "snake" shapes for raggedy hair. Break in 1½-inch strips and place on the clown.

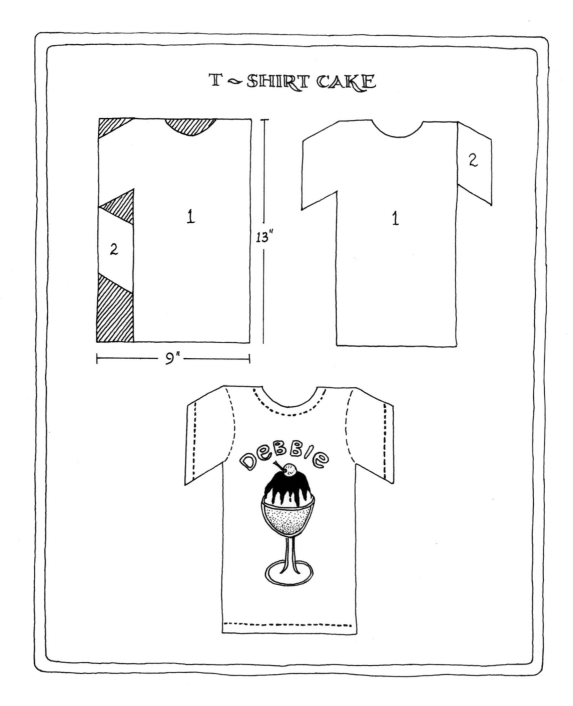

T ~ SHIRT CAKE

T-SHIRT CAKE

The T-shirt cake is great because of its popularity with young and old alike and because it is appropriate for either a boy or a girl. What's more, you can tie in someone's special interest—Batman or a popular rock group could be on the front of the cake, or the person's age, or a caricature or an ice cream sundae, or anything you can think of.

1. Bake a cake in an oblong pan of any size.
2. Make a serving board that's somewhat larger than your cake pan.
3. Cut a T-shirt pattern according to the illustration.
4. Cut the cake out according to the pattern.
5. Mix a batch of buttercream frosting (see p. 49)
6. Place piece 1 on the serving board and then place piece 2 for the other sleeve.
7. Frost the cake any color you want.
8. With frosting of a contrasting color in a No. 2 or 3 tip cone, draw stitching around the neck, sleeves and hemline.
9. Draw a design on the front. It may be something as simple as "Happy Birthday" or as elaborate as a map of the world!
10. I often work the age into the cake by adding a "Size 12" label in frosting in the neckline of the shirt. Stripes can be another colorful addition.
11. After you've finished with all the surface decorations, clean up the board around your cake and caulk the edge with a No. 6 tip cone.

TYPEWRITER CAKE

The typewriter-shaped cake is one of the easier cake sculptures. Once you learn a few basic techniques in cutting, filling in and building with cake, you'll probably want to design your own cake sculptures. But the typewriter cake is a good beginner's sculpture, and it fits many occasions for a secretary, writer or student.

When I left my job as a copywriter in the advertising business to open my cake shop, I baked my own farewell cake. On the paper area of the cake, I used a No. 1 tip cone to write the following lines: "I knew I was leaving so I baked a cake. This takes the cake. This is a piece of cake. This better not turn into one of my half-baked ideas! Now you take the cake."

If you know the particular typewriter the person uses, find its brand name

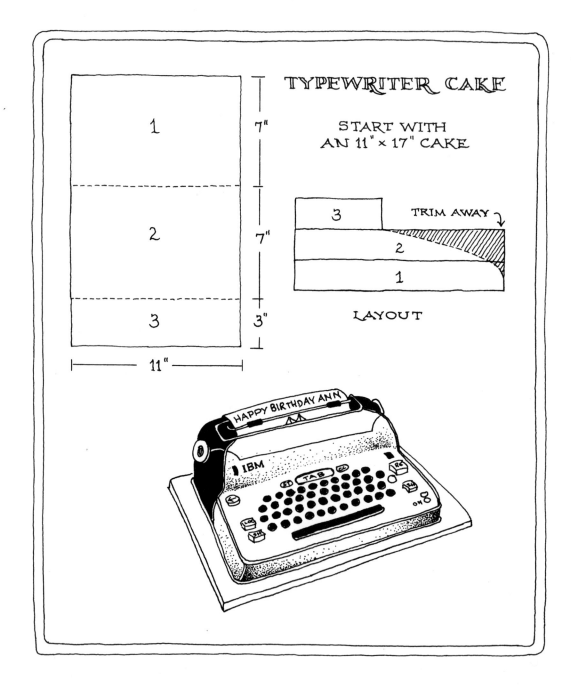

TYPEWRITER CAKE

START WITH
AN 11" × 17" CAKE

1 — 7"

2 — 7"

3 — 3"

11"

3

TRIM AWAY

2

1

LAYOUT

HAPPY BIRTHDAY ANN

IBM

TAB

in the yellow pages of your telephone directory and copy it someplace on the typewriter frame. That always adds a personal touch.

1. Bake an 11 × 17-inch sheet cake (8 cups of batter). Set it aside to cool.

2. Meanwhile, wrap a 14 × 12-inch piece of cardboard with white freezer paper for your serving board.

3. Prepare one recipe of buttercream frosting (see p. 49). Make a paper pattern according to the illustration, and after the cake has cooled at least an hour, cut it out, following the pattern.

4. Place piece 1 on your serving board.

5. Frost the back two-thirds of the bottom cake layer with buttercream frosting, using the cut raw edge as the back. (Generally, when I'm working with layers for my sculpted cakes, I spread uncolored buttercream or chocolate between layers rather than using a color.)

6. Place piece 2 on top, back edges together. If your cake is higher in the middle than on the sides, as often happens, shave away the higher parts of the cake as you layer your cake or else you will not end up with a level typewriter.

7. After you have the first two layers level, place the third and final piece on top.

8. Now take a long bread knife and shave the front two layers of cake so they form one slightly slanted surface. Compare your cake sculpture to the diagram. Once you have the slant where the keys will go, you're ready to apply the outside frosting.

9. Choose a color for your typewriter—say, yellow. Color enough frosting yellow to cover almost the entire cake, about two-thirds of what remains of your frosting mixture. You'll also need to color some frosting black for the carriage and some white for the paper insert.

10. With a yellow No. 5 tip cone, draw the outline of the top of the typewriter, as shown in the illustration. (I sometimes draw the outline of a piece of typing paper. If you plan where the other colors are to go, you won't end up with layers and layers of frosting, which when thick can be too sweet.)

11. Now fill in the carriage area with black or chocolate frosting. Fill in the paper area with white.

12. Finally, cover the rest of the cake with yellow.

13. Caulk with a No. 6 tip cone around the bottom edge next to the serving boards.

14. Now the fun begins. Color marzipan a light contrasting color—perhaps orange, or leave it off-white. This will be used for the keys. Roll the

marzipan out with your hands as though you were making a snake with clay. When the marzipan roll is about ⅜ inch in diameter, cut the roll into 55 or so pieces each ¼ inch thick. Gently mold each key into squarish-round shapes. Make three pieces slightly larger for the shift keys and the carriage return. Make one long piece for the space bar. And roll out a long piece for the cord and plug to make it "electric."

15. Now place the keys in four rows on the face of your typewriter and put the shift and space bars in place. With a dark-colored frosting—I usually use black—in a No. 1 tip cone, write the numbers, letters and punctuation marks on the keys. You should find a picture of a typewriter to make sure all the keys are labeled correctly and to get other details right.

16. You will also need two pieces of candy for the ends of your carriage. I alternate between rings made from marzipan and store-bought gumdrop rings.

17. Finally, decide what you want to write on the paper area of the cake. Something as simple as "Happy Birthday" may be perfect. The cake speaks for itself.

HAMBURGER CAKE

Imagine cakes that look like a hamburger, a slice of pizza, a slice of bread and butter, a wedge of Swiss cheese, a hot dog, spaghetti and meatballs, a chef's salad, a carrot, a banana or a triple-dip ice cream sundae. They've all been Creative Cakes because they're somebody's favorite food. The giant hamburger, complete with marzipan lettuce, cheese and tomatoes, is one of my personal favorites. So if you, too, have a burger king in your life, here's a fun idea for a cake that's quite easy and fun to make.

1. Mix enough batter of your favorite cake recipe to fill three 8- or 9-inch round pans. Bake and set aside to cool.

2. Wrap a serving board or find a round cake platter that is about a foot in diameter.

3. Prepare one recipe of buttercream frosting (see p. 49).

4. Add cocoa powder to buttercream frosting to make 2 cups of chocolate frosting. Add milk to the chocolate frosting a teaspoon at a time until it's easy to spread. This frosting will form your hamburger.

5. Color about another 2 cups of frosting with egg-yellow food coloring

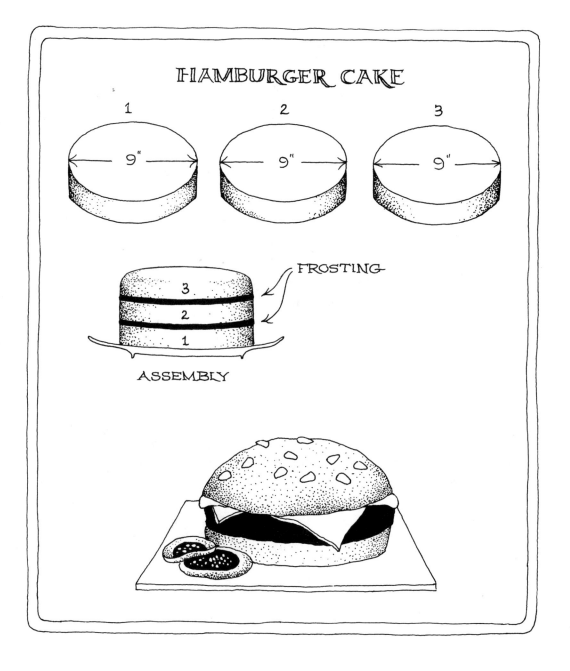

HAMBURGER CAKE

and a teaspoon or so of chocolate frosting until it's the color of a toasted hamburger bun.

6. Buy or make about 7 ounces of marzipan. Color half of it lettuce green by using yellow and green food coloring. Color portions of the remaining marzipan with red and egg-yellow for the tomato slices and the melted cheese, if you want them on your hamburger.

7. Assemble the three layers of cake one on top of the other, spreading frosting between the layers. If you find your cakes have risen too high in the center to make a flat surface, level them with a long bread knife before assembling. The top layer should be left rounded on top like a hamburger bun.

8. Carefully frost the sides of the bottom third of the cake with the light-brown-colored frosting, being careful to avoid crumbs. This is the bottom of the hamburger bun.

9. Next frost around the middle with chocolate frosting. Try to put this frosting on slightly thicker than the light-colored frosting so that it sticks out a little the way a hamburger does in a bun. However, don't make it too thick. You don't want it to slide down over the bottom frosting.

10. Now frost the top and sides of the cake down to the chocolate (hamburger) area with the light frosting. Smooth the top with a moistened knife. You may want to streak the top with a little dark chocolate frosting to give a toasted appearance.

11. To make your lettuce, roll the green marzipan as you would to make a snake with modeling clay. Now flatten it out with a rolling pin on waxed paper until it is about 1½ inches wide. Crimp the edges with your fingers to make it look like lettuce. Break off pieces about 3 inches long. Now stick them around and on top of the hamburger area of your cake. If you like, you can shape a couple of pickles out of marzipan, too.

12. If you want a cheeseburger, flatten the yellow marzipan and cut the pieces into triangles. Stick them into the side of the cake to look like melted cheese.

13. Finally, shape the red marzipan to look like the edges of tomato slices. Stick them appropriately in your cake. Or if you'd rather have ketchup, color some frosting red and let it ooze out the sides.

CHRISTMAS TREE CAKE

A three-dimensional Christmas tree cake makes a beautiful centerpiece for any holiday table. Unfortunately, a 3-D Christmas tree cake wastes more cake than most of my suggested cake designs because I've never seen a collection of small graduated round baking tins in which to bake the five layers needed for the cone-shaped tree. You may have. However, starting from a rectangular sheet and one round pan is easy enough, and you can always find someone to munch on your scraps.

1. Mix 11 cups of your favorite recipe. You may need to double your recipe. Fill one 11 × 17-inch sheet cake pan and one 8-inch round pan. Bake and cool.

2. Wrap a 12-inch square double thickness serving board or ready a sturdy cake platter or tray. Cut a 7½-inch circle from heavy cardboard.

3. Prepare one recipe of buttercream frosting (see p. 49).

4. Make a small amount of chocolate frosting by adding a tablespoon or two of cocoa powder to 1 cup of plain frosting. You may also need to add a teaspoon or so of milk. Drop a No. 8 tip into a parchment paper cone. Fill with chocolate frosting. Set aside.

5. You may want to select a variety of colored candies for decoration. M&M's, halved gumdrops and colored marzipan balls are perfect. Also, you'll need a box of white or yellow candles.

6. After the cake has cooled sufficiently, make patterns and cut the cake according to the illustration. I often simply trace round objects of the appropriate size (like container lids) right on the cake with a knife. You don't have to worry about making the circles exactly the specified size.

7. Place the 10-inch square on the serving platter. Frost with plain buttercream. Set aside.

8. Remove the 8-inch round cake from its pan and place it on the circle you cut. (This is the bottom of your tree.) Set the cake on your clean counter for assembly. Assemble the tree cake away from the base to avoid getting crumbs all over the base while you carve the cone-shaped tree. Stack the layers of cake, spreading frosting between each layer. When all layers are stacked, shave away the edges to make the cone shape. It is not necessary to have a perfectly smooth cone. Visualize a Christmas tree. Some jagged uneven edges will make your tree cake look more interesting and realistic. (If you're planning to do any traveling with your tree, you may want to cut a wooden

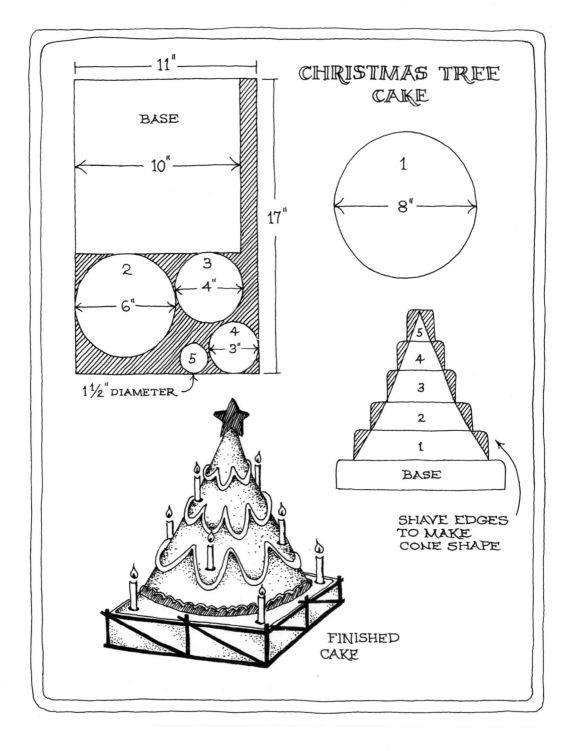

CHRISTMAS TREE CAKE

11"

BASE

10"

17"

1

8"

2

6"

3

4"

4

3"

5

1½" DIAMETER

5

4

3

2

1

BASE

SHAVE EDGES
TO MAKE
CONE SHAPE

FINISHED
CAKE

dowel the height of the tree to stick down through the middle of it to prevent the layers from sliding.)

9. Set aside about 2 cups of your remaining uncolored frosting. Color the larger portion green. If you are skillful at dabbing and spreading frosting without disturbing crumbs, carefully lift the tree with both hands and center it on top of your frosted square before you frost the tree. If you're not very skilled at spreading frosting, carefully frost the tree where you've assembled it. The tricky part of the procedure is setting the frosted tree on top of your frosted square. Here's the best method for accomplishing this: Place the base cake as close to the frosted tree as possible. Use a large nonpliable pancake spatula to lift the tree from the work surface. Steady your hand and lift it slowly. Guard the tree from toppling with your other hand. Don't worry about sticky fingers: it's easier to smooth the frosting and wash your hands than to salvage a fallen cake. Center the tree on the square base. Carefully slide the spatula out from under the cake while you are lowering it to the base. Avoid getting the spatula caught under the cake. You may have a tough time getting the spatula out without messing up the frosting on the base. You may need to touch up where you've had to hold the cake. Frost around the bottom of the tree and make sure no cake is showing.

10. Now you're ready to trim the tree. Either mix several colors of frosting with the remaining frosting and fill No. 2 and No. 3 tips and cones to draw on ornaments or use colored candies or both.

11. Draw a fence around the sides of the square with the cone filled with chocolate frosting. Using colored marzipan, shape miniature presents and toys to set around the tree. A teddy bear, tiny sneakers, a car, a truck or a ball are easy to shape.

12. Finally, stick a birthday candle in the top and all over the tree part of the cake. The cake is beautiful when it's all aglow. Just remember to light the candles starting at the top!

5

Thinking Creatively

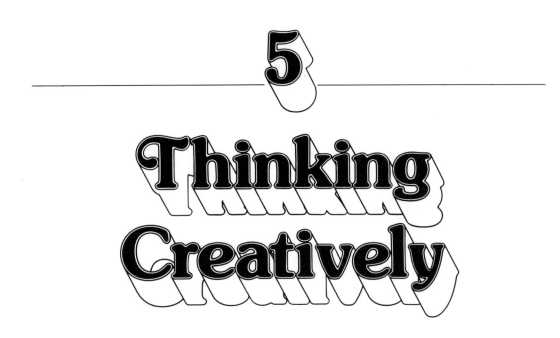

Coming up with an idea for your cake is probably the hardest part of creative cake baking. It takes time and thought to get the best ideas, which often and finally turn out to look the simplest. What's more, if your baking is limited to the same friends and relatives year after year, you may find it especially difficult to come up with a terrific idea every time. However, because everyone is so multidimensional and changes continually in his or her appearance, job, interests and preoccupations, soon you'll be able to capture all the different aspects of the special people in your life with your creative cakes.

Oftentimes people call me to place an order and say they have no ideas whatsoever. Moreover, if they are not familiar with my work, they have a hard time visualizing a style of cake decorating they've never seen. Usually after I have a probing conversation with those people who say they have no ideas, they can come up with some very creative concepts. People simply need a little leadership. In fact, you almost have to treat every cake as though it's a problem that can be solved by filling in the blanks of a questionnaire. So if you're having trouble getting started with an idea, perhaps the following list will help get you on the right track:

Name
Occasion
Theme of party
Hobbies
Job
Special Interests
Age
Favorite Food
Favorite Sport
Collector's Items
Favorite Fantasy
Unforgettable Experiences
Children

Before I take you step by step through the list, there are a couple of things I want to emphasize. First, try never to hurt anyone's feelings with your creativity. If you know someone has a sensitive spot, don't illustrate it in cake and embarrass him or her in front of twenty guests on his or her special day.

For example, one time the second anniversary of a couple who had barely made it to their first was approaching. The couple had separated, and rumors that they had filed for divorce were rampant. A customer told me the preceding story and went on to ask what ideas for a cake I could come up with to fit the occasion. She said she'd been wondering about a pair of boxing gloves! It seemed to me any type of cake would be in poor taste. I didn't accept the order immediately. Instead, I asked her to think about it. She never called back.

And before you make up a *Wall Street Journal* cake with a bunch of cutting headlines, be sure the stockbroker will take your ribbing in fun. While these headlines for Frankie D.'s thirtieth birthday are clever, they might hurt the feelings of an overly sensitive person: "Banker's Trust Raises Prime: Frankie D. Loses His." "Market Forms Double Bottom. Frank Forms Double Chin." "Dow Breaks 700 While Frank Breaks Down." "Frank Breaks 30: Market Yawns." In this case, Frank was such a tease, he deserved every comment. If you suspect that an idea goes too far, it's probably best to forget it.

And second, keep your cakes simple. When you make them too busy, they lose their impact. Many times there will be a lot of detail in a cake, but it should be subtle and carry out the theme. In other words, carry out one theme per cake. For example, a Monopoly board cake I once did for Parker Brothers was full of detail. Yet because I stuck to one theme, it was a terrific cake. I can't stress simplicity enough.

And now, on to your list:

Name

The cake idea may end with a name. If someone's name is short enough to spell out in individually cut-out letters, you can't get more personal. Especially, if the person has so many interests you can't zero in on one. For example, one time I did "L–I–Z" for a sweet sixteen. Liz was involved in tennis, music, school, boys, talking on the telephone, her family, cooking and about a dozen other things. No one of her interests took priority, which is a common dilemma for the creative cake decorator.

Since her mother had chosen blue-and-white-gingham tablecloths, we decided on the birthday girl's name cut out as the shape of the cake. It was decorated with cartoonlike illustrations of Liz doing all the things she likes to do. What looked like stitched-on patches of blue gingham were frosted on each letter. And navy-blue rickrack made from frosting outlined the letters at the border.

Another time, Rhonda had chosen plates and napkins for her sweet sixteen party that were a bright-colored floral pattern on a field of white. Her cake was her name cut out. The frosting decoration was the same pattern as the plates and napkins.

Joe, Brian, Kay, *Annie* (the show), and *People* (the magazine), just to name a few, have all been cut-out Creative Cakes.

Occasion

The main importance of the occasion for the cake artist is for the greeting inscribed on the cake. Oftentimes a birthday cake for one person may be the perfect anniversary cake for someone else. For example, on her birthday a secretary was once given a typewriter-shaped cake. Another time a typewriter went to Olivetti when a new model was introduced. And when Tony Hiss wrote a book about his father, Alger Hiss, the organizers of his press party ordered a typewriter cake—a replica in cake of the now-infamous Woodstock model.

The same typewriter could conceivably have been used in all three instances. Changing the inscription to fit the different occasions would have set them apart. The same applies to a state cake. It may suffice as a bon voyage cake for soon-to-be vacationers as well as for an appropriate birthday cake for the state's governor.

And aside from traditional holidays, birthdays, anniversaries, showers, weddings and graduations, consider other special occasions that deserve recognition, such as theater openings, office parties, housewarmings, mortgage burnings, job promotions and retirements. You will make every occasion more special with one of your creative cakes.

Theme

The theme of the party may open all sorts of ideas. Once my former employer, adman Jerry Della Femina, requested a luau birthday party. He'd become particularly fond of Trader Vic's that summer and asked them to cater the affair. It would have been inappropriate with such a dominant theme to give him a pencil- or typewriter-shaped cake, even though he's a writer. So the cake, which was the only surprise of the party, was a cut-out caricature of Jerry dressed as a Hawaiian dancer, grass skirt made from colored coconut and all. The only problem you may have with caricatures or portrait likenesses in cake is that if you know your subject well, your cake may begin to come alive on you. In fact, Jerry's comment when he saw his cake was "It looks more like me than I do."

Another time when the birthday boy's name was Jack, his wife decided to carry out his name as the theme of the party for his fiftieth birthday. She sent out invitations that referred to her "Jack of Hearts." The party room was decorated with all sorts of jacks: a jack for a car, playing jacks, Jack Daniel's whiskey, Jack Benny, Jack-o'-lantern, Union Jack, and on and on. When she came to me wanting to know what she could do for a cake, I suggested a jack-in-the-box, a three-dimensional job I could have done with the pop-out jack made from marzipan. The other idea I hesitantly offered was the jack of hearts, with husband Jack's likeness as the face. Picture cards make great-looking cakes, but I'd done them before, so I wasn't eager to do another one. I really wanted to do the jack-in-the-box; it would have been a much more interesting shape and a challenge for me. Nonetheless, with my recommendation known, she chose the jack of hearts to carry out the theme of her invitation. (P.S. I saved the jack-in-the-box idea for a couple of months. Eventually, a lady called wanting an idea for a christening cake. It was the perfect solution.)

You could serve a tennis racquet, tennis ball and sneakers cake at a tennis party. A tiger, lion and/or clown cake will liven up a circus theme. A pennant from either or both teams, a football or a helmet would be the perfect kick-off when the gang comes over to watch the Super Bowl.

Hobbies

It seems that everyone has a hobby whether it be growing bonsai trees, stock car racing, painting, cooking, gardening, needlepoint, bar-hopping, jogging, repairing old cars, or collecting Rolls-Royces! (You'd be amazed at the number of Rolls-Royce collectors among my clientele. Requests for the car became so frequent that I had to purchase an historical picture poster for reference that cost a small fortune in itself!)

An artist's palette is one of the easiest and most colorful cakes I've ever done—as is a chef's hat with a blue ribbon for *cordon bleu* cooking hanging from it. However, my favorite hobby cake was a needlepoint cake. Visualize a square canvas, partially completed. Short diagonal lines made with a frosting cone resembled yarn needlepoint stitches. The unfinished design read "Happy Birthday, Sylvia." In the bottom corners were two lion's heads. The significance of the lions was in her name, Sylvia Lyons. Again, marzipan added a nice touch. I made a needle and made it appear to be slipped through the needlepoint canvas with frosting strung through it as yarn.

Job

Some people are so enthusiastic about their jobs that it's the only way to depict them in cake—especially if it's the folks at the office who are doing the cake-giving. Again, the typewriter-shaped cake is a great-looking cake for anyone from secretary to novelist to manufacturer.

Or take a stockbroker. A job represented by stocks and bonds may seem like a boring way to say "Creative Cakes." However, if the broker is bullish, do a bull cake. If he's bearish, do a bear. Or why not combine both? If the broker is involved with the commodities market, perhaps a pig cake to represent pork bellies would be fun. Or a bag of potatoes cake. How about copying the front page of the *Wall Street Journal*, as was briefly discussed earlier? It has a nice typeface and always turns out to be impressive-looking once you've mastered lettering. Make up several headlines about the birthday broker. Indicate the rest of the copy with squiggly lines. The graph that is always part of the front page could read something like "Age on the Up and Up." By the way, any newspaper cake, whether it is your local daily or the *New York Times*, can be cleverly assembled.

In my New York operation, many occupations—doctors (a white coat cake with all the tools of the trade in the pockets, a huge thermometer cake, a stomach cake, a foot cake), lawyers (scales of justice, Lady Justice, an English barrister), carpenters (hammer, nails and saw), plumbers (wrench), race drivers (stock cars, boats, even an Indy car for Roger Penske), all manner of manufacturers (gloves, T-shirts, sweaters, dresses, blue jeans, shoes, cars, calculators, scissors, yarn, sheets)—have been represented by Creative Cakes. Hundreds of brand-name products from Meow Mix (one of my all-time favorite cakes) to Kellogg's corn flakes to Heineken beer to a Big Mac and French fries to Rolaids (not a good statement for a cake!) have also been Creative Cakes.

Special Interests

Some people have special interests that really wouldn't be considered hobbies. You should remember to consider such things as volunteer work, special studies and so on. You may come up with a clever idea if you do. Once for a fiftieth birthday, a woman ordered a cake cut in the shape of her husband dressed in a Boy Scout uniform—the summertime uniform with the shorts and knee socks. Her husband devoted much of his time to the Boy Scouts, not as a scout master but as a philanthropist. So the uniform was truly out of character for him, which is why the visual made a fun cake. He also had big feet—size 12, to be exact. So I gave the little boy cake great big feet!

Another time, an ambulance was ordered by a couple who was a member of a volunteer ambulance corps. Coincidentally, at the time of their anniversary, they were also expecting a baby. A pregnant lady drawn in frosting in the front seat of an ambulance driven by her husband was perfect!

Age

How old will the person be? Age can be a very important factor. If the person is a child of two or three, you are limited. What are the child's favorite toys? Does he recognize any particular cartoon or storybook character? One time a two-year-old who liked keys and cars was given a key ring (made from marzipan) with two keys (for two-years-old) and a car "hanging" on it. Another cake for a three-year-old who recognized the word "exit" every time he saw it was an exit sign!

When children are very young, their interests will change from day to day. So you can imagine how much they will change from year to year. Every birthday they will be infatuated with another cartoon character or TV star or toy (fire trucks, cars, airplanes) that can be designed into a cake. There are exceptions, however, such as six-year-old Adam, who has wanted nothing but a Batman cake for three birthday parties in a row!

I learned very early in my business that personal detail gets lost in cakes for the very young. Simply make them a cake in the shape of something they can recognize with a word they can say: Snoopy, Mickey Mouse, a pet, Big Bird. More ideas for children's cakes will be given later in the book.

In my New York City business, it seems the annual birthday party stops when children are ten. Then it's not until the bar or bat mitzvah, sweet sixteen, eighteenth, twenty-first, and such monumental birthdays as the twenty-fifth, thirtieth, thirty-fifth, fortieth, fiftieth, and upwards that people celebrate with big parties. As far as I know, the woman celebrating the biggest birthday with one of my cakes was Alice Roosevelt Longworth. When she was ninety-four, the former President's daughter was given a caricature of herself holding her pet Persian cat, Puss-Puss. The quote in the cartoon bubble coming from her mouth was from her favorite pillow: "If you don't have anything nice to say about somebody, come sit by me." The oldest man was Eubie Blake when he celebrated his ninety-fifth birthday with David Hartman on *Good Morning, America.* He was caricatured in marzipan playing ragtime on an upright piano cake.

Despite local customs, birthday freaks like me remember their friends every year by doing something special for them. No matter what some people say, I believe everyone wants to be remembered—and they should be. More than likely, you're one of those people, too. Warning: If you become compulsive about remembering birthdays, there will come a day when you'll forget someone. It won't be your fault, but you'll still feel terrible—as though you've failed at your job. Sometimes a specially decorated belated creative cake can save the day.

Getting back to the subject of the more celebrated birthdays, my untraditional bar mitzvah cakes have ranged from blue jeans to sneakers to skateboards to teeth with braces to portrait likenesses. Sweet sixteen cakes have been cars, T-shirts, caricatures, tennis racquets—anything depicting the teenager's special interest. The telephone has been the most popular sweet sixteen cake sending the right message to a talkative teenager.

Favorite Food

You'd be amazed at how many people are known to their friends and co-workers for the foods they eat! Charlotte Ford craves HoJo ice cream, so her sister Anne decided a cake shaped like an enormous chocolate ice cream cone would let her "eat her heart out." The folks at *Wonderama*, a children's television show, gave Toto the Monkey his favorite food for his birthday—a giant banana. It didn't fool Toto, though. He wouldn't go near the substitute for the real thing. (P.S. For those who may think tempting the monkey with a phony banana was an inhumane act, they also presented him with a big bunch of real bananas.)

Others who crave pepperoni pizza, Skippy peanut butter, Mallomar cookies, Big Macs, Hostess Twinkies, martinis, watermelon, Breyer's coffee ice cream, hot dogs, Hebrew National salami, Charles Chips, Snickers and even a chef's salad were also presented with cakes shaped and designed to look like their favorite foods. Any food product makes a great "pop-art" cake—even Kretschmer wheat germ!

Other fetishes besides foods make great cakes, too. For example, a person who conspicuously used Stim-U-Dents to clean his teeth was once given the package in cake. Another person who gave someone severe indigestion also gave him a Pepto-Bismol cake. Someone with a foot fetish was given a pair of feet! (Personally, I'm not keen on doing cakes in the shape of body parts, but in some cases, I can be bought! However, Creative Cakes does nothing pornographic. A little suggestive is as far as I'll go from time to time, but no private parts, if you know what I mean!)

Favorite Sport

If someone is a real tennis, squash or racquet-ball buff, a racquet and ball is always a hit. And since so many birthday parties are for the monumental years, such sayings as "30–Love" and "40–Love" are naturals, as well as "We love your racquet," "It's not your fault that you're 40," "You're a hit," "What a match, Love–40" (anniversary) and on and on.

By the way, you can think what you want about somewhat corny expressions, but they always get a chuckle. Puns and clever sayings often tie the cake and the occasion together. A few choice words give your effort the final touch. Just be careful not to be too contrived.

Golf bags make fun cakes, especially when the bag is the color of the golfer's. The pockets may be made from cake in relief. And the clubs may be sticking out from the end. Or else make a dog-leg fairway for a golfer. You can make the sand traps (granulated sugar and cocoa powder), weeded areas, lakes, bunkers and bridges from candies and gumdrop leaves. You can even make a tiny golf cart from marzipan.

Sneakers and golf shoes are also fun for the sport. Mainly because they're always oversized and look as though they were made for Paul Bunyan.

In New York, you're either a Yankee fan or a Mets fan—never the twain shall meet! A bubble-gum baseball card makes a fun cake. Also, a baseball mitt and ball are always safe for any baseball enthusiast.

A sporty cake I particularly liked was a pair of ice skates. Another time a skateboard was fun. And once I made a pickaxe and rope for a mountain climber.

Collector's Items

Collector's items will allow you to go on forever with cakes. Joey Heatherton collects elephants, so her office personnel gave her a cake shaped like an elephant. Sandy Dennis has a live cat collection, so a friend once gave her a cake made to resemble a big bag of Purina Cat Chow. Susan Fine collects pigs, so a pig cake. Another collector received an owl cake. And several shell collectors have been given giant shells. Antique matchboxes, old coins and prized cigar boxes have also been duplicated in cake.

However, my favorite collector cake went to a man who collects antiques. Many of his "real finds" have turned out to be costly duds, yet he still dreams of owning his own antique shop someday. His daughter granted his wish on a cake shaped as "Evans' Antique Junk Shop" containing all his prized possessions; a caricature of him was in the door.

Favorite Fantasy

Many times people have specific dreams you may know about. One travel agent longed to take the trip to Greece she'd sold so many times. So her friends at the office gave her a Pan Am ticket to Athens. The only thing it was good for, though, was dessert. A woman who fantasized having an affair with Robert Redford was caricatured holding a present with a tag reading "To Polly, Love, R. R." While another Robert Redford idol was hidden under the sheets with him in a bed-shaped cake. Robert Redford should only know how many requests I've had to paint his famous face on cake with frosting. Likewise, Dolly Parton has received similar popularity as a cake for an ogler of the opposite sex . . . "looking better than a body has the right." From all reports, though, none of these cake dreams have come true!

When Al Pacino was nominated for his outstanding performance in *Dog Day Afternoon,* he wanted the Oscar so badly he could taste it. Thanks to an adoring secretary, he did. She gave him a cake shaped like the treasured trophy for his birthday. And the following year she gave him a "two dog tags" cake, significant of his starring role in *The Basic Training of Pavlo Hummel,* for which he won a Tony.

Unforgettable Experiences

Is there anything funny the person would like to forget? Cartier, a prestigious jewelry store on Fifth Avenue, makes a distinctive black watch. As anything with class and popularity, the watch was copied by a company calling itself "Carlier." Of course, it sold for considerably less. The distinctive typeface used for Cartier's logo was used on the rip-off watch, as were the roman numerals. Last year for the president of Cartier's birthday, his co-workers presented him with a three-foot-long black watch-shaped cake with the *other* company's name on it, proving there's no present like the time! Another lady was reminded of a sqeamish experience with a marzipan mouse hiding in a high-heeled boot cake!

Children

Many mothers have practically devoted their entire lives to their families. Several times, appreciative children have gotten together and asked me to make a cake with all the children on it, copying a family portrait from years gone by. One time a lady gave me a picture of the house in which her family grew up. The cake was in the shape of the house, and we had the five children climbing all over it. Another time I did the old woman in the shoe, with all the children and grandchildren in the different windows.

One time a loving husband came by with no ideas. Nothing we came up with seemed quite right. Suddenly he noticed a *Time* magazine cover I had in my reference collection. It was the week when the Total Woman made the cover, depicting a housewife's many chores from diapers to dishes to lover. "That's my wife!" he exclaimed with relief. So that magazine cover became a Creative Cake.

With thousands of cakes in my past, I could spend all my time describing them to you. However, I'd rather help you create some new ones. Therefore, I hope these experiences will be enough to help you get your head spinning with ideas.

Once more, I can't impress upon you enough how important it is to keep your ideas related to one theme. There will be times, however, when a person has many interests, with no one outstanding. The best way to illustrate that problem is with a funny caricature of the person bogged down with all his interests and perhaps his favorite expression in a cartoon bubble. Or, as I once did for a multitalented woman, make a caricature of the person wearing and surrounded by many different appropriate hats.

Other helpful aids for ideas are magazines. When you're stumped, simply paging through a magazine may spark a thought. You should also consider starting a picture file of airplanes, cars, trucks, famous people, sports, cartoon characters and everything you might want to refer to when you're making a cake. Picture books and encyclopedias are also great references. Children's books are particularly good because their illustrations are simple.

A dictionary with color plates and a world atlas will also come in handy. In fact, I'm always referring to the yellow pages! It's chock full of company logos and pictures and typefaces. I often think I should write Ma Bell and thank her for compiling such a terrific reference book.

So now you've got it. A step-by-step method to help you come up with a cake idea for any special occasion—and even some occasions that aren't so special!

6

Some Food for Thought

CHILDREN'S CAKES

Children's cakes are probably the most fun. First, they are usually brighter and simpler than adult cakes and therefore meet my criteria for the best creative cakes. And second, children will *appear* more excited over your creations than older folks. It's probably just their enthusiasm, but it works. Children really make you feel rewarded for your efforts.

Coincidently, cakes for elderly people usually produce the same results. It's those in-between years that often find people too sophisticated to share their true feelings with you! Perhaps that's not being fair to the hundreds and hundreds of people who have called me and written me in thanks for a job well done. But how can "thank you very much for a delicious cake" compare to a little girl who in thanking me for her Holly Hobbie cake wrote: "All my friends stuck their fingers in my cake when I wasn't looking." Or the little boy who wrote in wonderment that it must have taken me "five days" to make his airplane cake. Or the other little girl who wrote that she would "let" me make her cakes every year. That was three years and three cakes ago! One mother sent me a note saying her three-year-old slept with the picture of his Batman cake for over a week!

The letters from the kids are precious. No two ways about it. And they make you feel special, too. And while *all* my wonderful letters are dear to me and are what keep me going when I've worked too many hours or am feeling a little low, the letters from children are the one I'll always remember.

With one exception, christening cakes have been the earliest cakes I've made for children. (One time a lady who'd just given birth ordered a huge baby bottle for her newborn baby to give to the nurses who watched over him.) I've stayed away from christening cakes for the most part. As I've said, my cakes are usually bright. A christening seems like such a chaste affair that most people still prefer to be traditional. However, one idea that works nicely for a christening is to decorate a rectangular sheet cake to look like a sampler. With pastel colors, use a No. 1 tip to make cross-stitch letters spelling out the baby's name, birth date, weight and other vital statistics. Also, greeting cards such as those by Betsey Clark or ones designed especially for christenings often have delicate designs you can copy.

Another time I made a jack-in-the-box. The jack was sculpted and molded from marzipan. The face and the polka dots were added decoration from frosting. The box was a seven-inch cube of cake. The four sides of the cube were frosted and decorated to look like a child's building block—a big letter J for the child's name, Jay, on one side; a train engine on another; a bluejay on another; and the name J–A–Y spelled out in blocks on another. The top was made from marzipan a couple of days before so it would be hard enough to stand alone. I loved that cake!

One mother brought me a wall plaque of the rabbit from *Alice in Wonderland* that hung in her baby's nursery. She wanted her baby's cake to be cut out in the same shape and design. The rabbit was holding a clock, so we set the clock at the baby's time of birth. And the scroll in the other hand included all the other specifics.

The first birthday is a big celebration in New York. I've been amazed. In my personal experience growing up in Indiana, I don't remember ever celebrating first birthdays with a big party. In New York, it's quite an affair— I remember one first-birthday party where fifty adults and ten children were going to be served Creative Cake after the Omelet Man had performed his edible act!

First-birthday cakes are best, again, when simple. Designs from Snoopy to blocks to a truck to a train to any toy or thing the child might recognize will suit the occasion. Even a big number 1 with the child's favorite things works nicely. (The number 1 is also a simple shape for the less experienced decorator.)

The true joy of children's birthdays begin when the child is two or three. By this time, a child has begun to develop a personality and the exchange among the children at the party becomes a special treat in itself. Also, the birthday cake will have meaning to the child.

Moreover, by the age of two or three, children have distinctive likes and dislikes. Television personalities from Captain Kangaroo to the Sesame Street gang to cartoon characters are perfect ideas for cakes as well as things they may love. One three-year-old yelled "Volkswagen!" every time he saw one on television or on the street. His mother ordered a yellow Volkswagen for him, telling me the real test of my ability and success would be if he yelled "Volkswagen!" when he saw his cake. He did! Children always have been my best critics!

Some of my favorite cakes have been designed by children with little guidance from me. Jodi was a Brownie the year of her eighth birthday. The week before her party, she arrived with a Brownie doll and a picture of herself. I made the cake look like a Brownie Jodi doll. The following year the same clever child had grown up and become infatuated with Donny Osmond. So this year she requested a cake of Donny and her. This time she brought me several fan magazines from which to copy a likeness of her idol. And she gave me such memorable details as his favorite color, purple, and his catchy expression, "cute," to work into the design.

Other favorites of kids are the superheroes. Superman, Wonder Woman, Batman and Robin, Spider-Man are frequent requests.

Since the phenomenon of *Star Wars,* R2D2, the little droid, has achieved great popularity as a cake. He's fun either cut out flat for the beginner or standing up for the more skillful decorator. He has knobs and gadgets that can be made from marzipan and other candies. Be imaginative. R2D2 certainly is.

A good source of ideas is to consider what's going on in the movies, on television and at school. One child loved school so much his mother presented him with a school bus cake. Another decided a blackboard with the message: "Do your homework" was the most pertinent idea for her ten-year-old. And still another helped me create a messy room for a sloppy son. They really wanted him to clean up on his birthday!

Listing favorite cake ideas for children will only give me the opportunity to leave many out. Nonetheless, the following are among the most frequent requests: rocket, car, truck, fire truck, sneakers, tennis racquet, hockey stick and puck, football, baseball mitt, skis and boots, T-shirt, silly socks, Snoopy, Raggedy Ann and Andy, ballerina, a pet. I hope one of these will spark the perfect idea for your youngster's next birthday.

ANNIVERSARY CAKES

Anniversary cakes often present an immediate problem because you have to find a way to represent both members of the couple in cake. Many times the couple has totally different interests. The only thing that ties them together is their children. And while putting all the children on a cake is one way you could solve this problem, there are other ways.

For example, if you know how many years the couple has been married, you could do as John Clark and Lynn Redgrave did for their tenth anniversary. The tenth anniversary gift is tin—though John Clark informed me the diamond industry is trying to push the diamond since so few couples are together for their sixtieth anniversary! So we decided to make the cake resemble a huge box (the cake was for a hundred guests) of aluminum foil. The cake read, "Tin happy years, Lynn and John," and was otherwise decorated with all the particulars of an aluminum foil box.

The list of wedding anniversary gifts on page 108 may help you come up with a clever idea. A fourteenth anniversary? What says "ivory" in cake?

Elephant tusks? Possibly. But why not a big pop-art cake that looks like Ivory soap?

ANNIVERSARY	TRADITIONAL	MODERN
First Year	Paper	Clocks
Second	Cotton	China
Third	Leather	Crystal
Fourth	Books	Appliances
Fifth	Wood or Clocks	Silverware
Sixth	Iron	Wood
Seventh	Copper, Bronze or Brass	Desk Sets
Eighth	Electrical Appliances	Linens, Lace
Ninth	Pottery	Leather
Tenth	Tin, Aluminum	Diamond Jewelry
Eleventh	Steel	
Twelfth	Silk or Linen	
Thirteenth	Lace	
Fourteenth	Ivory	
Fifteenth	Crystal	Watches
Twentieth	China	Platinum
Twenty-fifth	Silver	Silver
Thirtieth	Pearl	Diamond
Thirty-fifth	Coral, Jade	Jade
Fortieth	Ruby	Ruby
Forty-fifth	Sapphire	
Fiftieth	Gold	Gold
Fifty-fifth	Emerald	Emerald
Sixtieth	Diamond	Diamond
Seventy-fifth	Diamond	Diamond

Also, you could copy the couple's wedding picture, as I did for Mr. and Mrs. Dom Vitaliano on their golden anniversary. (I mention them here by name because Mr. Vitaliano came out of retirement to paint my tiny shop when I was first setting up Creative Cakes in 1974. Thanks to him, his time and his energy when I was busy doing a hundred other things, I had no worries whether or not I'd be ready for my opening-day party. He's also responsible for the cement step out front that says "Creative Cakes 1974." I always want him to know how much I appreciate him.)

Anyway, a fifty-year-old wedding picture was really dated, as you can imagine. Wedding-dress styles had definitely changed, as had the couple! It made a terrific-looking cake, all in sepia colors. There were no color pictures back then. The caption read: "The first fifty years are the hardest. Happy Anniversary."

Another way to go is to make caricatures of the husband and wife. In one instance, the husband awakened every morning at five-thirty to jog for half an hour before breakfast. His wife was a golfer and designer of women's golf attire. Their cake was a man in a blue sweatsuit and sneakers holding an alarm clock set appropriately. And a women in a golf dress (one she had designed) holding a golf club in one hand and a heart with all the children's names in the other. It made a happy twenty-fifth anniversary cake.

If you are skilled at painting with frosting, a technique where you use a small frosting spatula instead of a brush, you can copy a picture to create a portrait likeness of the couple in cake. This has been a very popular cake at Creative Cakes and is really one cake I can't teach you on paper. You must develop your own style for portrait cakes, the way any portrait artist does. Moreover, with this cake design, you must consider cutting it up. People sometimes tell me later they were unable to slice up the heads. And that their cakes were carefully frozen in their freezers! Would you want an eyeball staring you in the face from a dessert plate? (That problem can easily be solved by smearing the face with a spatula just before serving the cake if it really bothers you!)

One particular instance reminds me how you can add a little humor to the otherwise serious portrait cake. The husband was almost as fond of peanuts as he was of his wife. So at the bottom of the cake, you could see the top of a bag of peanuts in his hand. The wife was picking one out of the bag. The peanuts brought the couple together once again.

But if you're really stumped for an idea, you could do something as simple as a heart-shaped cake. You could make the heart look like a patchwork pillow—make tassels from red licorice laces—and decorate the patches with different significant things about the couple. Or simply decorate the heart with all the names of their children. Or perhaps just their two names: "Don + Carol, 30 Happy Years."

HOLIDAY CAKES

Once you get involved in cake art, you'll take advantage of every special occasion to display your handiwork. Perhaps you'll want to start by welcoming in the New Year with Father Time. Or maybe make a cone-shaped cake decorated to look like a party hat with a noisemaker alongside of it.

And if you allow a groundhog cake to escape your creativity on February 2, be prepared for Valentine's Day. This is an easy one. A heart is perfect. Or you may want to select a valentine from a card shop and copy it on a cake.

You'll find many beautiful designs, which will allow you to be as simple or as elaborate as you want.

Don't be afraid to copy other artists' designs. It does *not* mean you are any less of an artist. It's simply a way to develop your talent. Artists have done it since day one. When I was a youngster I can remember wondering how artists come up with so many designs—how could they possibly have all those pictures in their heads? It never occurred to me until I was grown up and working in advertising just how much illustrators and art directors use other artists' work for ideas, reference and detail.

So why not copy a penny for Lincoln's birthday? Or cut out a cake in Lincoln's profile? Or copy a quarter or a one-dollar bill for Washington's?

In the spring, let the Easter Bunny find his way to your table. Or a little yellow chick. Or make one of my favorite cakes, an Easter basket. Fill it with jelly beans and other Easter candy. Make the grass from colored coconut. You'll have fun being creative with this one!

Graduation is another time to give cakes as gifts. If you've mastered the art of lettering with frosting cones, get your hands on a diploma from the graduate's school. Copy it. It's always impressive. Or design a cake representative of the graduate's field of study: a doctor's white coat or a little black bag; a lawyer's scale of justice or lawbook; a plumber's wrench; a vet's cat or dog; an MBA's briefcase; a teacher's blackboard. And on and on and on.

An American flag will always raise the spirits on the Fourth of July as will a big slice of watermelon. Or why not a big firecracker? You can make the fuse with a licorice lace.

Caspar the Friendly Ghost or a not-so-friendly ghost makes an easy cake at Halloween. Greeting cards, again, are full of fiendish characters from witches to goblins as inexpensive ideas to copy. Or make a cake that looks like a Halloween mask. Use leftover pieces of cake to make the nose stick up in relief. Cut out holes for eyes. Use licorice laces for the elastic that holds the mask on.

A turkey cake, a horn of plenty, or pilgrims are welcome sights at Thanksgiving. A couple who announced their engagement on Thanksgiving was presented with their likenesses dressed in pilgrim clothes. He'd hidden her diamond ring in a cannoli when they dined at their favorite Italian restaurant when he popped the big question. So she was holding a pastry box of cannoli in her hand.

And finally, Christmas. There are so many parties at Christmastime that you can keep yourself really busy if you want—and even busier if you give your cakes away as gifts. A Christmas stocking can be personalized and stuffed with all sorts of goodies. A Christmas tree can be flat or three-dimensional. A

Christmas card. A Santa Claus. A wreath. Or anything with a Santa's hat or a wreath adorning it. There are so many ideas for you to come up with at Christmas. And a creative cake makes a colorful and festive addition on your otherwise traditional dessert buffet.

HOLIDAYS AND CELEBRATIONS

New Year's Day • January 1
Groundhog Day • February 2
Lincoln's Birthday • February 12
Valentine's Day • February 14
Washington's Birthday • February 22
St. Patrick's Day • March 17
First Day of Spring • March 20
Easter Sunday
April Fool's Day • April 1
Mother's Day • Second Sunday in May
Memorial Day • May 30
Flag Day • June 14
Father's Day • Third Sunday in June
First Day of Summer • June 21
Independence Day • July 4
Labor Day
First Day of Autumn • September 22
Jewish New Year • October 2
Columbus Day • October 9
Halloween • October 31
Veteran's Day • November 11
Thanksgiving
First Day of Winter • December 21
Chanukah
Christmas • December 25

CITIES, STATES AND COUNTRIES

Cities, states and countries make interesting cakes and generally are easy shapes to decorate, depending on how elaborate you make the finishing touches. My Creative Cakes have ranged from very simple Floridas and Austrias for winter vacationers to a more detailed New Hampshire for a wedding cake, from a Los Angeles road map for a bachelor party to a very developed New York State for the governor's birthday.

What I like to do is to copy the topography of the land if there are mountain ranges, rivers and lakes. Also, I always indicate major cities and the ones of significance for the occasion. If the place is known for something special—Florida for its sun, for instance—you can draw pictures and other pertinent details and special attractions that set that particular place apart from all others. It's also fun to make little cars, airplanes, moving vans and boats from marzipan to set on top of your cake for dimension.

So all you do is find a map—here's where an atlas or an almanac is a definite help. Make a paper pattern in the outline of the city, state or country. To take you a step further, consider New York State, as I did for one of Governor Hugh Carey's birthdays. A world almanac will provide you with such information as its nickname, the Empire State; its motto, "Excelsior, Ever Upward"; its flower, the rose; its bird, the bluebird; and its tree, the sugar maple. I used all this information on the cake in addition to the personal information given to me that would distinguish the cake as the governor's: Niagara Falls, the Adirondacks, Lake Placid, site of the 1980 Winter Olympics, a state rose garden, the governor's Shelter Island home, Long Island ducks, the capitol building at Albany and a commuter plane to the Big Apple—all stood up in three-dimension.

ZODIAC SIGNS

These days with so many people following their stars by reading their horoscopes the moment they pick up the newspaper or their favorite magazine, the zodiac signs are often appropriate and interesting shapes for birthday cakes. The zodiac sign is also a good way to solve a cake idea when several people are honored at the same birthday party: the one thing they all have in common is their horoscope.

The *Farmer's Almanac* is a good and inexpensive reference book complete with line illustrations of all the zodiac signs and the varying traits characteristic of each sign. It's a fun book in its own right just to have around. It usually has some interesting recipes, too.

Aries—The Ram • March 20 to April 19
Taurus—The Bull • April 19 to May 20
Gemini—The Twins • May 20 to June 21
Cancer—The Crab • June 21 to July 22
Leo—The Lion • July 22 to August 22
Virgo—The Virgin • August 22 to September 22

Libra—The Balance • September 22 to October 23
Scorpio—The Scorpion • October 23 to November 21
Sagittarius—The Archer • November 21 to December 21
Capricorn—The Goat • December 21 to January 20
Aquarius—The Water Bearer • January 20 to February 19
Pisces—The Fish • February 19 to March 20

MINI CREATIVE CAKES

Leftover pieces of cake can be creative, too. There's no need to simply throw them away. Before or after the unveiling of your creative masterpiece, treat your family and friends to frosted leftovers. Label them just as they are with such words as "edge" or "scrap" or "corner" or "mmmm—good." Or perhaps write a different name on every piece. Everyone likes to see his name in print!

If you have large enough pieces and you have the time to go to a little more trouble, do as I often do and make mini creative cakes. They're ideal to freeze and keep for a rainy-day surprise. (By the way, if you want to freeze unfrosted scraps for some reason, follow the freezing instructions on p. 33.)

One mini-cake that now seems to me to be the perfect use of cake scraps is the first mini-cake idea I ever had: decorate the leftover pieces of cake to look like a piece of cake. That's right, a piece of cake. I still remember how proud I was the day I made that first mini-cake. Why I hadn't thought of the idea before, I'll never know. The "piece of cake" mini-cake was such a natural and obvious way to go, and as it turned out, it was relatively easy to do.

Here's all you do: Consider a wedge shape. I usually begin with a 5-inch square of sheet cake on the bottom and a 5 × 2½-inch layer on top. You'll have to shave some cake away to give the wedge a perfect slant. Piece the cake together where you must. You'll need chocolate and white buttercream frosting—about two cups of each (see pp. 49 and 51). Frost the slanted area and one of the sides with the chocolate frosting. Frost the other two sides with white frosting. Take a knife and run white frosting down the center of the chocolate as though to separate two chocolate layers of cake. There you have it. A creative cake that looks like an oversized wedge of chocolate layer cake is as easy as one, two, three. I usually write "You take the cake" on it. And when I put a "Mini Creative Cakes for Sale" sign in my shop window, that's exactly what my customers usually do with them!

I've also been known to take a wedge of cake and frost it with yellow frosting to look like a wedge of Swiss cheese. That's the only way I've ever made a cheesecake! So I usually write, "Say *cheesecake*" on it, and it gets a smile. Sometimes I even go a step further and sit a marzipan mouse on top.

Another idea for leftover pieces is a strawberry. Piece your sizable scraps together and mold and shave them into a strawberry shape. Cover with red frosting. Use black frosting in a No. 3 tip cone to make dots all over. You can make a leaf by flattening a green gumdrop with a rolling pin and cutting it to a leaf shape with your scissors. That way, if you love strawberries, they'll always be in season.

A light bulb shape frosted with white buttercream and a contrasting color in a No. 5 tip cone for the screw-in end makes a cute cake when you write "Watt's for dessert?" on it.

Or how about making a tiny sneaker? a peanut? a banana? a tiny tennis racquet? a slice of watermelon? or a miniature football? "Pass the dessert!"

Again, when you use your imagination, your leftovers will be as much fun and as creative as your cakes.

7

Cakes I Have Known

GRIMSBY/BEUTEL

The end of 1975 reunited a popular news team on WABC-TV, Channel 7, one of the local stations in New York City. Della Femina, Travisano and Partners, an advertising agency, handled the WABC-TV account. On this particular occasion, as the agency so often does, they ordered a cake for their client, who was having a big send-off luncheon for the team at the Plaza Hotel.

The cake they ordered was a copy of a press photo used in the promotion of Roger Grimsby and Bill Beutel's being together again. And as with any portrait likeness cake I do, it's not one I knock out in an hour or two. It's a lot of work.

Anyway, the cake was picked up by a messenger, and I assumed all went well until later that afternoon, when I received a phone call from Mark Yustein, an art supervisor at the ad agency. With a note of panic in his voice, Mark asked, "Did you hear what happened to the cake?" My heart sank. I figured Roger didn't favor his likeness in cake. Mark went on to tell me that after a fine reception, they decided not to cut the cake. Instead, they decided it should go back to the newsroom, where the hard-working people who made the show possible could eat it. And perhaps enjoy cutting up two big cut-ups. Another messenger was called to make the delivery. And the cake, which was in a 28 × 18 × 5-inch box, was carried away—*underneath* the arm of the messenger the way you'd carry a big suit box! The messenger claimed no one told him it was a cake or that it must be kept perfectly level—this despite the Creative Cakes logo stamped all over the box.

Between our laughter and my disbelief, Mark told me the messenger service had volunteered to pay for the damages of the cake. And then he asked me when I could make another one.

I've always prided myself in having a job where I didn't have to do the same thing twice. That's what makes cake art fun for me. But this time I was caught off guard. As I looked at my schedule, I almost begrudgingly told him I could fit it in the following week. But the cake date was postponed until the following week because of the Christmas holidays. Finally, when the cake was finished a second time, the wife of the owner of the messenger service appeared with check in hand to personally deliver the cake to the newsroom. This time when it arrived, Roger Grimsby intercepted it. He just happened to be having a party the following evening, and *he* wanted to use it. Anything to please Roger!

Postscript: About six months later Joan Lunden and Roger Sharp, two reporters for WABC-TV, were in my shop working on a cake story for the seven o'clock *Eyewitness News.* Roger noticed the Grimsby/Beutel promotion cake in one of my albums. "You know something?" he asked. "That cake was around for weeks. First it was at the luncheon for Roger and Bill at the Plaza, and then it showed up a couple weeks later at a party at Roger's."

SUPERMAN

The superheroes make great looking cakes. Batman and Robin, Wonder Woman, Spider-Man and Superman have all been Creative Cakes again and again. And adults enjoy them as well as children. Two thoughtful and loving boys once gave their mother a Wonder Woman cake. The cake spoke for itself. One wife whose husband read Spider-Man in the funnies before he read the front page of the newspaper wanted a cake in the image of Spider-Man without his mask, thereby revealing a likeness of her husband's balding head. The cartoon blurb read: "Don't tell anyone I'm 34 and still into Spider-Man." Superman has been the image several wives have had for their multitalented husbands. However, one special occasion for a Superman cake will always be among my favorite cake stories.

One morning a petite lady who was about eight months pregnant stopped by my shop for her appointment. Her husband's thirtieth birthday was coming up, and she needed a cake. She saved me a lot of time and creative thinking because she knew exactly what she wanted: Superman. And because her husband had been recently crazed by tennis, she wanted her Superman to be holding a tennis racquet. That was it—simple as that.

Whenever a customer comes in absolutely sold on an idea, there's always a story behind it. And usually a good one. Considering her delicate condition, I thought maybe that had something to do with the choice of Superman. But as always, I did not want to leave anything to chance. So I asked, "Why Superman?"

She laughed for a second, blushed, then continued in her embarrassment to shyly tell me the story about their honeymoon. As it turned out, her husband, foreseeing a possibly tense situation, wanted to add some comic relief to their wedding night. When she came out of the bathroom dressed in her new negligee, he was waiting for her "more powerful than a locomotive" dressed in a Superman suit.

I got a big kick out of the story and hoped her husband would be equally amused when reminded of the incident in front of fifty guests.

The day of the party I received a phone call from Mrs. Superman telling me her husband would be by to pick up the cake late in the afternoon. Since the design of the cake was a surprise, she asked me to keep it a secret by sealing up the box before he got there. No problem there, unless, as Superman, this Superman imposter had X-ray vision!

Probably even more amusing to me than the incredible wedding-night episode was the image I created in my mind when a man as small in stature as his wife walked into my shop to pick up his cake. All I could imagine was this slight man standing on the bureau of the honeymoon suite in a Superman suit ready to make his leaps and bounds. It's a vision that still makes me chuckle.

MOLLY MAE

Pet cakes are big sellers for children. Therefore, when a lady called one day to see if I could make a cake shaped as a springer spaniel for her five-year-old, I didn't think it was a strange request. The lady made an appointment to bring me pictures of her springer spaniel. That was that.

Several days later an elegant-looking lady in a beautiful full-length mink coat walked into my tiny shop. Elegance is always noticed when it enters my country-style shop, as it seems so out of place alongside me in my apron. Anyway, the woman introduced herself as Molly Mae's mother, and went on to add she was the lady interested in a cake shaped as a springer spaniel. She'd brought me photographs to copy.

I began filling out the order as I always do, getting such particulars as name and phone number. Every other word out of her mouth was how important this fifth-birthday party was going to be.

Then I asked for the correct spelling of Molly Mae. And I went on to ask if Molly had any other special interests aside from her dog. Only then did I learn that Molly Mae *was* the dog. A show dog was being honored on her fifth birthday by a party with fifty people guests. I was a bit taken aback. It was a red-letter day for Creative Cakes. I was going to make my first birthday cake for a dog. Well, a pet dog, anyway!

At any rate, I got all the other information I needed such as the date of the party and how many of the fifty guests the cake was to serve. Then I gave her a price. As she was paying her deposit, she whipped open her coat. There embroidered in the lining of her gorgeous mink was "Molly Mae's Mother." Moreover, not only had dresses been made from the same blue chiffon for Molly Mae and her mother, but Molly had been practicing to hold a cake knife for the cake-cutting ceremony!

Postscript: The morning following the party I received a phone call from Molly's mother. She thanked me for the "perfect likeness" of Molly Mae and then asked me to hold on because someone else wanted to thank me. I prepared myself for an "arf, arf." However, this lady full of surprises didn't let me down. She handed the telephone to her husband, who also expressed his gratitude and best wishes.

ANNIVERSARY PORTRAITS

Ruby Green was planning a big thirtieth wedding anniversary affair at the St. Regis Hotel. As so many ladies do, she'd brought her family album with her when she arrived to select her Creative Cake. During our twenty-five-minute meeting, she told me many adoring things about her husband, shared with me in pictures their thirty years of marital bliss, their worldwide travels, their three children, and their active involvement in their community. She wanted it all on her cake!

As I've mentioned throughout this book, simplicity is best. Personally, I don't think cakes with everything in the world on them are impressive. They seem cluttered to me and oftentimes pompous. Nonetheless, my customers are paying me to do what they want. I can only advise. So we compromised. Since the party was so large—a hundred and fifty guests had been invited—the base of the cake would be a layered rectangular sheet. On top of the frosted sheet would be another cake: cut-out portrait likenesses of the anniversary couple. The background would include the busywork illustrations of all the wonderful things they'd done in simple one-color line drawings, so as not to distract any more than possible from the center of attention, the celebrating couple.

The photograph Mrs. Green had chosen to reproduce on the cake turned out to be black and white. So while we were talking, I began making color notations on my order sheet. First, she described her husband to me. Brown hair and blue eyes. Brown plaid suit and pale yellow shirt. Brown tie. Then I looked up at her and wrote down her hair and eye color. No sense asking. There she was. "Blond bouffant hair and hazel eyes," I said aloud to myself.

"No," she replied.

Startled, I looked up again. Perhaps her eyes were blue. "What do you mean?"

Mrs. Green pointed to her hair. "It's a wig. I always wear wigs. Sometimes I wear my black one. Or my brown one. Or my red one. Or like this, blond."

She continued to explain she hadn't yet decided which wig she was going to wear the evening of her anniversary party. So she didn't know what color to tell me to make her hair on her cake. She said she'd have to call me at a later date, closer to her party.

I thought for a moment, wondering how my good intentions would be received, before I asked, "If all your friends know you wear wigs, why not let me color your hair in as many different hair colors as you have wigs? It's your personality, isn't it?"

Mrs. Green loved the idea. So on the evening of Ruby and Morty Green's thirtieth wedding anniversary, Ruby was all wigged out in multicolored hair in Morty's embrace.

Later, Mrs. Green wrote me that the cake was delicious and that they'd had a lot of fun with it. And that's really what I want Creative Cakes to always be. Fun. Just plain fun that's always in good taste!

NANCY DUSSAULT

Nancy Dussault has had more cakes made especially for her than any one person during any two-and-a-half-year period. Two and a half birthdays, you may wonder? Not exactly. Nancy's case is a prime example of the different occasions—seven, to be exact—you may find for creating special cakes. Nancy has been an acquaintance through a mutual friend for as long as I've lived in New York City. So she knew about my cakes long before Creative Cakes was actually a business.

However, it was not until my first summer in business that she had her first occasion to receive one of my special cakes. Nancy was doing summer stock in New Jersey, starring in *Irene*. A piano plays a major part in that production, so on her closing night, a friend ordered an upright piano cake with Nancy dancing on the keys. That cake taught me you must remember to check every detail. Perhaps check it twice. When I had last seen Nancy, she had had shoulder-length hair—the way you may remember her as the neighbor in *The Dick Van Dyke Show*. When Nancy stopped by to pick up her cake on the way to the evening's performance, she had since had a haircut—a really short haircut. Nancy-on-the-piano still had long hair!

Then a few months later she make her debut as hostess of the new *Good Morning, America,* with David Hartman as the host. This time the same friend sent her a "Nancy Wake Up" cake. Alongside her bed (a three-dimensional one, with a headboard, pillows and figure beneath the ND monogrammed sheets) was a night stand. On the night stand was a tiny alarm clock made from marzipan, ringing that early-morning hour of five o'clock. A Yorkshire terrier (Nancy's was named Winston) was pulling the covers off the bed, trying to awaken her.

That cake will always be memorable not only because I got carried away in the fun of creating all the miniature details, but more so because my job didn't end when the cake was decorated. I'd been asked to deliver it as a personal favor to our mutual friend, who was away in California on business. He wanted Nancy to have it before her opening on the show. His secretary provided me with the address and preferred time of delivery.

So I got myself out of bed on this particular Monday, my day off, at 5:30 A.M. I then headed for the ABC studios by taxi. I arrived at a skyscraper on Broadway and 66th Street, and a guard watched me go up to the seventh floor, cake box in hand. No sooner had the elevator shut behind me than I discovered that the door was locked in front of me. Where was everybody? Where was the show? I rang for the elevator. It didn't come. I knocked and knocked at the door in front of me, certain I could hear voices from within. As seven o'clock neared and I was panicking because I'd not successfully completed my mission before the show was to begin, I pressed the elevator key again. Still I could arouse no one. How long was I going to be stuck on the seventh floor? Finally, about twenty minutes later the elevator came. The guard told me he'd gone out for coffee. He also explained he didn't know why he had allowed me to go up—he knew all along the *offices* were not open at that hour! There I was, having been given the office address instead of the studio. The surprise was ruined. Finally I was so disappointed I just left the cake with the guard. A phone call later confirmed Nancy had received it before the end of the day. And Nancy, always seeing the brighter side, said she probably appreciated it more after she'd got over the jitters of her opening day.

In January 1976, I made my *Good Morning, America* television debut. And Nancy got another cake. Only this time she helped decorate it. It happened to be the birthday of W. C. Fields on January 29, so I decided to decorate a cake in his honor, since nearly everyone would recognize the wisecracking gentleman. I had partially decorated the caricature before I arrived. During the eight-minute segment, Nancy added a few details while I explained what I'd done and what she was to do.

When Nancy and I had finished with W. C. Fields, red nose and all, I presented Nancy and David Hartman with a personalized television-shaped cake—they were both on the picture screen with *Good Morning, America* coffee mugs. That appearance started a relationship with *Good Morning, America* that has given me some of my most precious and cherished memories. *Good Morning, America* has been very good to Creative Cakes.

Back to Nancy. Her birthday is June 30. In 1976, it came amidst the bicentennial celebration of America's birthday. So I designed a caricature of Nancy wearing a dress resembling Old Glory. She was saluting as the cake sang "Happy Birthday to our All-American Girl."

Then on the first anniversary of the show—I couldn't believe the year had passed so quickly—came another order. And while Nancy was not the sole recipient of the cake, her efforts were among those celebrated as the *Good Morning, America* logo was reproduced in honor of a triumphant first year.

Several months later, much to my disappointment, Nancy left the show to continue her acting and singing career. Yet, it presented me with another challenging job as the folks from the show wished her a fond farewell. This time I did an almost life-sized three-dimensional cake of Nancy's Yorkie, Winston. (God rest his soul. Old age took him to Dog Heaven shortly thereafter.) A personalized bowl (also a cake) was filled with candy and placed in front of the dog cake. The caption read as though Winston were speaking: "It's been a dog's life. Finally, we don't have to get up at 5:00 A.M. anymore."

Lastly, Nancy opened on Broadway in *Side by Side by Sondheim* in the fall of 1977. During a radio interview promoting the show, I overheard her sniffling and complaining of a cold. It gave me a perfect opportunity to wish her success in the show and thank her for all the customers she'd sent my way. I made her a personally decorated Kleenex box cake (stars, musical notes, and a caricature of Nancy I copied from the newspaper adorned the box) with a pop-out tissue made from light-blue-colored marzipan.

I doubt if the cake did much good for Nancy's cold, but considering the remedies available, she assured me it was as good a cure as any!

LIFE AT THE AGENCY

My business is very personal. Oftentimes I become extremely familiar with my customers from the questions I have to ask to get ideas. In one particular instance, the customer is an advertising agency. It's a small agency and I've come to know most of its employees, not personally, but through their cakes.

And since in this instance, most of my communication with them is over the telephone, I wouldn't know most of them if I saw them. But as you read on, you'll see just how much I've learned about the personality and growth of this agency from making cakes to suit its special occasions.

For example, one winter one of the partners spent six weeks on crutches after a skiing accident. One of his favorite pastimes was playing the horses for fun and profit. A horse on crutches made a very amusing cake! And also a fitting symbol of his success as a handicapper.

The other partner is known for his untidy office. The latest report was that he didn't get the hint when the folks at work gave him a Mr. Clean cake for his birthday.

And when the office manager had her birthday, the staff presented her with an Elmer's Glue cake and a greeting: "Thanks for helping us stick together."

Then there was the three-month search for a competent secretary. When they finally found one who could both answer the telephone and take a message at the same time, they thanked her with a big yellow Life Saver cake.

Another time three copywriters shared the same birthday. They also shared the same typewriter cake.

Darts is the agency sport. Gin rummy is the agency card game. You guessed it! Both a dart board and a gin rummy hand have been cakes.

And when one of the partners' two school-age sons became the agency messengers for part of their summer vacation, they were given an off-to-camp cake in the shape of the messenger assignment slip. It was filled out to fit the occasion. "Nepo" and "Tism" had requested the order!

And finally, when they moved to new quarters on the day of two employee birthdays, they celebrated with a flatbed moving truck carrying a big traditional-type birthday cake.

I can't imagine what they'll do next; but I'm looking forward to helping them celebrate whatever it is.

FORTUNE COOKIE

Oftentimes I purchase props or brand-name products before I design my cakes. It saves time and prevents my making mistakes or forgetting important details. For example, imagine something as simple as an artichoke. You've seen it a thousand times, but try to draw it from memory so someone will look at it and immediately say "artichoke." That's why I invest in props.

There's a shelf over the door of my shop with hundreds of such props. I sometimes catch customers examining my odd collection. It really amuses me to know they are wondering why in the world everything from J. C. Penney Motor Oil to Mop & Glo to Aramis to Dove to Elmer's Glue to Preparation H is in a cake shop.

The guys in the liquor store on the corner get a kick out of my business, too. In the beginning, whenever someone ordered a cake for an occasional nipper who favored a specific brand, I would leave a deposit and borrow whatever I needed. When I was finished, I'd return the bottle along with a box of cake scraps. It wasn't until I showed them a couple of pictures of my spirited cakes that they thought I was legitimate. These days they don't require the deposit!

On one particular occasion, a husband had ordered a fortune cookie–shaped cake for his wife. She was a reporter at *Fortune* magazine and his nickname for her was Cookie. The fortune, partly exposed on the outside of the cookie cake was to read, "Confucius say: Fortune's Cookie have happy birthday." Easy enough and a clever idea, I thought. What's more, it would be an interesting shape to sculpt.

What made this a memorable cake was the conversation I had at the Chinese take-out restaurant right around the corner from my shop. The managers knew me well. One time I went on a spareribs kick that lasted twenty-two days in a row! Anyway, I walked in and before they could say "spareribs?" I asked if I could buy "just *one* fortune cookie."

A guy standing at the counter reading the menu looked up and with an expression of disbelief and concern asked, "Are things really that bad?"

BRICKS AND WHEELBARROW

People are always asking me how I come up with so many clever ideas. What those people must realize is I'm operating my business in what I can't help but consider the most creative city in the world. New York continually regenerates my ingenuity. What's more, every one of my customers is different—even different from year to year. So there are millions of ideas with which to work.

Plus, as soon as two people begin to brainstorm, it's much easier to come up with original ideas. A sounding board helps trap creativity much faster. That's how my customers help me and vice versa. After a few simple questions, even customers who at first have said that they have no ideas come up with unique and interesting concepts.

However, some of my favorite cakes have been ones that took very little creative thought but rather depended on my creative execution of someone else's idea. For example, one of my cleverest customers was a lady planning a birthday party for her husband, who is a mason contractor. His most recent construction job was a high-rise apartment building made from brown bricks. Evidently, the job had taken considerably longer to complete than expected. And the big brown building was known around their home as more of a headache than anything else.

Mrs. Mason called one day to see if it were possible to have a cake made in the shape of a pile of bricks. I agreed that it could be done, but that I didn't think it would make a very interesting-looking cake on the white board I'm accustomed to using for my cakes. She thought for a moment and then said, "What if you made the cake fit in a wheelbarrow?"

My instant thought was that it would take an awful lot of cake to look like anything in a wheelbarrow. But I loved the idea. So I responded. "Yes, if it's a child-size wheelbarrow." We were set.

The day before her party, she delivered a green wheelbarrow she'd purchased from a toy store. The wheelbarrow was about 20 by 12 by 5 inches. I built up a mound of cake, frosted it with chocolate between layers and placed it inside the wheelbarrow. Then I sculpted the block of cake until it looked like a random pile of bricks. I prepared the rest of the frosting to match the model brown brick. And frosted the sculpture, being careful to square the corners. On one side of every brick was "Jim–40," his name and age. And what looked like rope made from frosting was strung around the bricks with a name tag, also designed from frosting, reading "Happy Birthday."

When Mrs. Mason came to wheel her cake home, she told me she'd also gone to an ice cream store where she had buckets filled with soft ice cream. She planned to serve the ice cream with a mortar spreader. That's really laying a good foundation for a party!

Postscript: Mrs. Mason called the morning after her party to say the bricks were a big hit, but when an enormous present to the husband from some mischievous friends unwrapped to reveal a real live voluptuous naked lady, she felt more like throwing the bricks than eating them.

A SPECIAL CAKE STORY

Creative Cakes has given me a life full of surprises. More surprises and opportunities to meet interesting people than I ever imagined I'd experience. You'll probably appreciate some of what's happened to me if I give you a few insights about me. First of all, I don't read *Women's Wear Daily* or "Suzy Says" regularly. I've never been a loyal follower of any of the daily gossip columns. *People* magazine satisfies my hunger for gossip every other week or so. But since I'm not a native New Yorker, even when I do read the society columns, very few names mean much to me.

Anyway, in time people began sending me lovely notes thanking me for cakes I'd created. Other people would come in and recognize a signature and act impressed. Many times, until someone pointed it out, I was unaware that one customer was any more socially well known than another. And as I consider it, it's a good thing I don't know everybody. If I did, I'd probably be so nervous and excited all the time that I couldn't concentrate and do my best job—such as the time I did a congratulatory cake for Frank Sinatra and his new bride Barbara Marx when they were visiting the Robert Wagners. I was so wound up the cake took me forever!

And on another occasion, a birthday cake for the late Joan Crawford took a long time, too—not in decorating so much, but in the time I wasted on the telephone telling all my friends about the order! Joan Crawford was such a *big* star.

So at times I get affected. Even though I have a business where *every* order is special, I occasionally find myself treating some customers more specially than others.

Sometimes I can't help it. It's difficult not to when I've been chauffeured with my cakes to parties in Glen Ridge, New Jersey, for Ron Travisano, and to *The Mike Douglas Show* in Philadelphia to help Totie Fields celebrate a birthday. David Hartman, Chita Rivera (she even called all the way from Canada once to order a cake for Liza Minnelli!), Budd Calisch, and Stuart Levin are among my most faithful customers. Cicely Tyson has sent me beautiful flower arrangements every time she has placed an order! Richard Avedon sent *me* a photograph of him with his cakes. Dick Clark took time from his busy cross-country schedule to personally thank me for his cake. Martin Charnin often orders cakes for the cast of *Annie* when a member has a birthday. And on and on and on. Heather Bernard of WNBC once said my list of clients read like *Who's Who in New York*. I keep calling my life vicarious. But all these people have really been part of it. They help keep me in business. And they certainly make my life more interesting.

For instance, one time about three years ago, a lady calling herself Mrs. Forstmann phoned to set up an appointment to see me. She'd been recommended by Susan Fine, one of my first and still best customers. A few hours later a pretty, unassuming lady arrived at my shop. She told me her cake problem: her husband was having a birthday and she wanted a crossword puzzle cake. She'd been to an engagement party for Phyllis Cerf and Mayor Robert Wagner when I'd done one. She hoped I could make one up for her, too.

"Sure. I love to make up crossword puzzles" was my response. So I began getting information for clues. As Mrs. Forstmann began running through her list—Ferrari, Mercedes, tennis, golf, Sun Valley, London, Charlotte—I interrupted only once to ask the correct spelling of "Ferrari."

I still don't know which clue triggered her identity. Maybe it was the combination of the clues and of wondering who this lady was who had attended a party for the Robert Wagners where other notables such as game-show wizard Mark Goodson had been. But suddenly, the clues revealed to me that Charlotte Ford Forstmann, fashion designer from the Ford automobile family, was sitting across from me. And even in Muncie everybody has heard of Charlotte Ford.

As an afterthought, I often chuckle at a comment made by another customer who noticed one of Charlotte Ford's cakes in one of my albums. "Boy! You really have some famous customers. What's it feel like to do cakes for the President's wife?"

8

Last Chapter

Once your cakes become the hit of every party and you are known as a cake artist, your friends and friends of friends may begin asking you to create one of your clever and delicious treats whenever there is a birthday. If that happens, and you begin to feel abused and resentful because things are getting out of hand, it may be time to consider charging for your cakes . . . but that's another book.

Chances are, your cake art will never turn into a full-time business. Instead, it will grow into a wonderful and gratifying hobby that will allow you to express yourself with cake whenever you feel like it. And whether or not you create cakes for profit, for years to come your greatest reward will be surprising your friends and relatives with your masterpieces and seeing their delight in your thoughtfulness that will give every special occasion a personal touch.

My love for cake decorating has gone beyond that. I no longer know every person who receives one of my cakes. I know all about them. You can be sure of that. In fact, you wouldn't believe what some people tell me about their friends. But that, too, is another book. I'm seldom around when my works of art are presented. Consequently, I've replaced the thrill and anxiety of presenting my cakes to my friends with the thrill of watching the creative process at work. It's gratifying to help my customers come up with ideas that I get to turn into personalized cakes fit for the occasion. It's really a special feeling to know I'm responsible as I watch people get excited when they see the result of their ideas in one of my cakes. And while it's true I'm not in love with all my cakes, I'm in love with the planning, thought and time that has gone into every one.

Since thousands and thousands of cakes have gone out the doors of Creative Cakes, you can certainly imagine all the fun I've had earning a living in my little business. My only regret is that I can't go inside my cakes sometimes. Many of *my* favorite creative personalities have been gifted with my cakes. And other times when I hear the guest list at a particular party, I'm proud that my Creative Cakes have been among those honored.

Undoubtedly, operating my Creative Cakes in New York City exposes me to a cross section of people like no other place in the world. The presence of the Broadway theater as well as radio and television headquarters brings me a big celebrity clientele most cities don't have. Celebrities add a special touch to my business. It's funny. Many people I've looked up to all my life are suddenly looking to me for their cakes. And it really makes *me* feel great when someone of great success receives one. However, the greatest thing about people everywhere is that *we're all* unique. There are as many cake ideas as there are people—even more, because people, as well as occasions, change from year to year.

It is my hope that *Creative Cakes* has given you some good ideas. It's not supposed to be the end-all, though. It's simply the beginning. Once you start creating cakes for your family and friends, there will be no limit as you extend your creativity from cake to cake. Just remember to keep notes and to take pictures of all your cakes. Someday you'll get a kick at looking at all the progress you make. And for years to come you'll enjoy one of the greatest hobbies in the world.

Index

About the Author

STEPHANIE CROOKSTON has been baking since her childhood in Muncie, Indiana. In 1974 she opened her cupcake-sized shop called Creative Cakes in New York City. Since then, she's created over 4,000 original cakes and counts among her customers such notables as Cicely Tyson, Roger Grimsby, Chita Rivera and Dick Clark. Stephanie and her cakes have made a number of television appearances and have featured in a variety of publications including *New York* magazine, *People* and *Ladies' Home Journal*. *Creative Cakes* is her first book.